Landmarks of world literature

George Eliot

MIDDLEMARCH

Landmarks of world literature

General Editor: J. P. Stern

Dickens: *Bleak House* – Graham Storey
Homer: *The Iliad* – Michael Silk
Dante: *The Divine Comedy* – Robin Kirkpatrick
Rousseau: *Confessions* – Peter France
Goethe: *Faust. Part One* – Nicholas Boyle
Woolf: *The Waves* – Eric Warner
Goethe: *The Sorrows of Young Werther* – Martin Swales
Constant: *Adolphe* – Dennis Wood
Balzac: *Old Goriot* – David Bellos
Mann: *Buddenbrooks* – Hugh Ridley
Homer: *The Odyssey* – Jasper Griffin
Tolstoy: *Anna Karenina* – Anthony Thorlby
Conrad: *Nostromo* – Ian Watt
Camus: *The Stranger* – Patrick McCarthy
Murasaki Shikibu: *The Tale of Genji* – Richard Bowring
Sterne: *Tristram Shandy* – Wolfgang Iser
Shakespeare: *Hamlet* – Paul A. Cantor
Stendhal: *The Red and the Black* – Stirling Haig
Brontë: *Wuthering Heights* – U. C. Knoepflmacher
Pasternak: *Doctor Zhivago* – Angela Livingstone
Proust: *Swann's Way* – Sheila Stern
Pound: *The Cantos* – George Kearns
Beckett: *Waiting for Godot* – Lawrence Graver
Chaucer: *The Canterbury Tales* – Winthrop Wetherbee
Virgil: *The Aeneid* – K. W. Gransden
García Márquez: *One Hundred Years of Solitude*
  – Michael Wood
Cervantes: *Don Quixote* – A. J. Close
Céline: *Journey to the End of the Night* – John Sturrock
Boccaccio: *Decameron* – David Wallace
Wordsworth: *The Prelude* – Stephen Gill
Eliot: *Middlemarch* – Karen Chase
Hardy: *Tess of the d'Urbervilles* – Dale Kramer
The Bible: – Stephen Prickett and Robert Barnes

GEORGE ELIOT

Middlemarch

KAREN CHASE

Department of English, University of Virginia

The right of the
University of Cambridge
to print and sell
all manner of books
was granted by
Henry VIII in 1534.
The University has printed
and published continuously
since 1584.

CAMBRIDGE UNIVERSITY PRESS

Cambridge

New York   Port Chester   Melbourne   Sydney

Published by the Press Syndicate of the University of Cambridge
The Pitt Building, Trumpington Street, Cambridge CB2 1RP
40 West 20th Street, New York, NY 10011-4211, USA
10 Stamford Road, Oakleigh, Melbourne 3166, Australia

First published 1991

Printed in Great Britain at
the University Press, Cambridge

British Library cataloguing in publication data
Chase, Karen *1952–*
George Eliot.
1. Fiction in English. Eliot, George, 1819–1880
I. Title   II. Series
823.8

Library of Congress cataloguing in publication data
Chase, Karen, 1952–
George Eliot, Middlemarch / Karen Chase.
    p.   cm. – (Landmarks of world literature)
Includes bibliographical references.
ISBN 0–521–35021–2 (hard) – ISBN 0–521–35915–5 (pbk)
1. Eliot, George, 1819–1880 – Middlemarch. I. Eliot, George,
1819–1880. Middlemarch. II. Title. III. Series.
PR4662.C47   1991
823′.8–dc20   90–26692   CIP

ISBN 0 521 35021 2 hardback
ISBN 0 521 35915 5 paperback

GG

Contents

Chronology

	George Eliot's life and work	Historical and literary events
1819	Born as Mary Anne Evans, 22 November, daughter to Robert Evans and Christiana née Pearson, the youngest of five children	Peterloo massacre; Queen Victoria born; Byron, *Don Juan* I–II; Shelley, *The Cenci*; Scott, *Ivanhoe*
1820–1	Family moves to the nearby village of Griff. Mother gives birth to male twins who live only ten days	George III dies and George IV accedes to the throne; House of Lords addresses the case of Queen Caroline; Malthus, *Principles of Political Economy*; Keats, *Lamia*; Shelley, *Prometheus Unbound and Other Poems*
1822		Death of Queen Caroline; Faraday discovers principles of electromagnetic rotation; James Mill, *Elements of Political Economy*; Shelley, *Epipsychidion and Adonais*; Suicide of Castlereagh; death of Shelley; Royal Academy of Music founded
1824	With her brother Isaac, GE attends Mrs. Moore's dame school at Griff House, and then is sent to join her sister Chrissey at Miss Lathom's boarding school	Death of Byron; *Westminster Review* founded; Landor, *Imaginary Conversations* (–1837); Coleridge, *Aids to Reflection*; Scott, *Redgauntlet*; Repeal of Combination Acts; Hazlitt, *The Spirit of the Age*
1826	With her father and mother travels from home for the first time, visiting Derbyshire and Staffordshire	
1827		Keble, *The Christian Year*; death of Beethoven; death of Blake; Thomas Arnold becomes Headmaster of Rugby; The Duke of Wellington becomes Prime Minister
1828	Attends Mrs. Wallington's school where she is exposed to strong Evangelical influences	University College, London opened

Year	Life	Historical and cultural context
1829		Catholic Emancipation Act; Carlyle, "Signs of the Times"
1830		William IV accedes to the throne; Lyell, *Principles of Geology*; Tennyson, *Poems, Chiefly Lyrical*; Cobbett, *Rural Rides*
1831		Carlyle, *Characteristics*; cholera epidemic; Mill, J. S. "The Spirit of the Age";
1832	Attends the Miss Franklins' school in Coventry; engages in wide reading in the English literary tradition	First Reform Act; deaths of Bentham, Goethe, and Scott; Goethe, *Faust II*; Tennyson, *Poems*
1833		Beginning of the Oxford Movement; *Tracts for the Times*; (–1841); Carlyle, *Sartor Resartus* (–1834); abolition of slavery in the colonies; Browning, R., *Pauline*
1835	During a period of ill health for both her mother and father, leaves the Miss Franklins' school	
1836–7	Her mother dies; GE becomes father's attendant and housekeeper after Chrissey marries and leaves home	First train in London (to Greenwich); Pugin, *Contrasts*; Dickens, *Pickwick Papers*; Queen Victoria accedes to the throne (1837); Carlyle, *History of the French Revolution*; Dickens, *Oliver Twist* (–1839)
1838–9	Travels to London with her brother Isaac; studies Italian with Joseph Brezzi; begins to prepare a chronology of ecclesiastical history; writes poems; reads Christian treatises and the poetry of Wordsworth	

George Eliot's life and work	Historical and literary events
	Marriage of Queen Victoria and Prince Albert; establishment of the Penny Post
1840 In January her first published work, a short poem, appears in the *Christian Observer*; begins the study of German; buys Keble's *Christian Year*; reads Byron's *Childe Harold*, *Don Quixote*, Tasso, and Isaac Taylor's *Ancient Christianity*	
1841–2 With her father moves to Foleshill; begins important friendship with Charles and Caroline Bray; reads Charles Hennell's *An Inquiry into the Origins of Christianity*; displaying her new distance from former religious enthusiasm, refuses to accompany her father to church; writes to her father, disavowing belief in the Divine authority of the Scriptures: "I regard these writings as histories consisting of mingled truth and fiction"; endures the anger, confusion and resentment of her family	Newman, Tract 90; Carlyle, *On Heroes, Hero Worship and the Heroic in History*; *Punch* founded
1843 Travels to Malvern and Wales with the Brays and Sara and Charles Hennell; meets Robert Owen	Wordsworth becomes Poet Laureate; Carlyle, *Past and Present*; Mill, *System of Logic*; Ruskin, *Modern Painters* (–1860); Dickens, *A Christmas Carol*; *Martin Chuzzlewit* (–1844)
1844 Undertakes to complete Rufa Hennell's translation of *Das Leben Jesu* by D. F. Strauss; visits a phrenologist to have her character read	
1845 Declines proposal of marriage from unnamed young painter; finishes the second volume of *Life of Jesus*; meets Harriet Martineau; travels to Scotland with the Brays	Newman converts to Roman Catholicism; Irish famine; Disraeli, *Sybil*; Engels, *Condition of the Working Class in England*; Fuller, *Woman in the Nineteenth Century*

Year	Life	Historical and cultural context
1846	In June *Life of Jesus* published; writes series of reviews for the *Coventry Herald*	Repeal of the Corn Laws; Lord John Russell becomes Prime Minister; beginning of commercial telegraph; Lear, *Book of Nonsense*; Thackeray, *Book of Snobs* (–1847)
1847	Nurses her father, travelling with him to Isle of Wight; reads Richardson's *Sir Charles Grandison* with great enthusiasm	Communist League founded; Brontë C., *Jane Eyre*; Brontë, E., *Wuthering Heights*; Thackeray, *Vanity Fair* (–1848)
1848	Reads George Sand's *Lettres d'un voyageur*; approves of the political revolution occurring in France; meets Emerson who writes, "That young lady has a calm, serious soul"	*The Communist Manifesto*; Revolutions in Europe; Chartist Petition; Pre-Raphaelite Brotherhood founded; Gaskell, *Mary Barton*; Kingsley, *Yeast*
1849	The death of her father in May; goes abroad with the Brays, travelling through France, Italy and Switzerland; settles in Geneva until the following spring; takes lodgings in Geneva with D'Albert-Durade, a painter	Bedford College for Woman established; Macaulay, *History of England* (–1861); Mayhew, *Labour and the Poor* (–1850); Ruskin, *The Seven Lamps of Architecture*; Dickens, *David Copperfield* (–1850); Brontë, C., *Shirley*; Arnold, *The Strayed Reveller and Other Poems*
1850	Returns to England in March; resolves to live in London as a writer; writes a review of R. W. Mackay's *The Progress of the Intellect*, published in January of the next year in the *Westminster Review*	Death of Wordsworth; Tennyson becomes Poet Laureate, *In Memoriam*; restoration of the Catholic hierarchy in England; Dickens begins to edit *Household Words*; Browning, E. B., *Poems*; Browning, R., *Christmas Eve and Easter Day*; Wordsworth, *The Prelude*
1851	Takes a room at 142 Strand, the home of John Chapman; in May Chapman buys the *Westminster Review*; her relation to Chapman brings objections from Chapman's wife; meets Herbert Spencer and G. H. Lewes	The Great Exhibition in Hyde Park; Meredith, *Poems*; Ruskin, *The Stones of Venice* (–1853); Gaskell, *Cranford* (–1853)

George Eliot's life and work	Historical and literary events
1852	Reviews Carlyle's *Life of John Sterling*; waxing and waning of her close emotional tie to Herbert Spencer to whom she was rumoured to be engaged; in the autumn visits Harriet Martineau in the Lake District	Death of the Duke of Wellington; Newman, *University Education*; Thackeray, *Henry Esmond*; Dickens, *Bleak House* (–1853); Arnold, *Empedocles on Etna and Other Poems*
1853	Reads Gaskell's *Ruth* and Brontë's *Villette*; moves to 21 Cambridge Street; abandons editorial role on the *Westminster Review*; friendship with Lewes matures	Brontë, C., *Villette*; Gaskell, *Ruth*; Thackeray, *The Newcomes* (–1855); Maurice, *Theological Essays*; Arnold, *Poems*
1854	Translates Feuerbach's *Das Wesen des Christen-thums*, published in July as *The Essence of Christianity*; begins liaison with Lewes, with whom she travels to Weimar and then to Berlin; Lewes writes his *Life of Goethe*; scandal in London over their relationship	Crimean War (–1856); London Working Men's College founded; Dickens, *Hard Times*; Gaskell, *North and South* (–1855); Patmore, *Angel in the House* (–1863)
1855	Returns to England in March and resumes her active career in intellectual journalism	Livingstone discovers Victoria Falls; Palmerston becomes Prime Minister; *Daily Telegraph* founded; Dickens, *Little Dorrit* (–1857); Kingsley, *Westward Ho!*; Trollope, *The Warden*; Browning, R., *Men and Women*; Tennyson, *Maud and Other Poems*
1856	Completes a translation of Spinoza's *Ethics*; she and Lewes request that she be known as "Mrs. Lewes"; writes several important essays, including "Worldliness and Other-Worldliness: The Poet Young," "The Natural History of German Life," and "Silly Novels by Lady Novelists"; in September begins her life as a writer of fiction with "The Sad Fortunes of Amos Barton"	Froude, *History of England* (–1870)

1857	*Amos Barton* in *Blackwood's*; M. A. Evans takes the name George Eliot; finishes "Mr. Gilfil's Love Story" in April and immediately begins "Janet's Repentance"; in October begins writing *Adam Bede*; objecting to her life with Lewes, her brother Isaac breaks off communication with her	Indian Mutiny; Buckle, *History of Civilization in England* (–1861); Thackeray, *The Virginians*; (–1859); Trollope, *Barchester Towers*; Browning, E. B., *Aurora Leigh*; Gaskell, *The Life of Charlotte Brontë*; Hughes, *Tom Brown's School Days*
1858	Reveals the identity of "George Eliot" to Blackwood; through the year her incognito is increasingly jeopardized; finishes *Adam Bede* in November	Carlyle, *Frederick the Great* (–1865); Trollope, *Dr. Thorne*; Morris, *The Defence of Guenevere and Other Poems*
1859	Lewes' *Physiology of Common Life* published in January, *Adam Bede* in February; spread of rumour that one Joseph Liggins is the author of *Scenes* and *Adam Bede*; finishes "The Lifted Veil"; begins *The Mill on the Floss*; abandons the secrecy of her authorship; Dickens sends high praise of *Adam Bede*	Franco-Austrian War (–1861); Darwin, *The Origin of Species*; Smiles, *Self-Help*; Mill, *On Liberty*; Dickens edits *All the Year Round*; *A Tale of Two Cities*; Collins, *The Woman in White*; Meredith, *The Ordeal of Richard Feverel*; Fitzgerald, *Rubaiyat of Omar Khayyam*; Tennyson, *Idylls of the King* (–1885)
1860	After finishing *Mill* in March, she and Lewes depart for Italy where he suggests Savonarola as the basis for the novel that would become *Romola*; returns to England in July, where she writes "Brother Jacob" in August and begins *Silas Marner* in September	*Essays and Reviews*; unification of Italy; Ruskin, *Unto this Last*; Dickens, *Great Expectations* (–1861); Trollope, *Framley Parsonage* (–1861); *Cornhill Magazine* founded
1861	After publication of *Silas Marner*, another trip to Italy for more historical research leading to *Romola*; ill during the trip; demoralized at the slow progress of the new novel	American Civil War begins; death of Prince Albert; Reade, *The Cloister and the Hearth*; Hughes, *Tom Brown at Oxford*

	George Eliot's life and work	Historical and literary events
1862	Writes and rewrites the opening of *Romola*; decides to publish it in *Cornhill* (for seven thousand pounds) instead of *Blackwood's*; publication begins in July; visit from Browning in December	Colenso, *The Pentateuch Examined* (–1879); Meredith, "Modern Love"; Browning, E. B., *Last Poems*; Braddon, *Lady Audley's Secret*
1863	In June *Romola* finished after long exertion: "I began it an old woman, – I finished it an old woman"; she and Lewes purchase The Priory at Regent's Park where they move in November	Founding of the Football Association; Huxley, *Man's Place in Nature*
1864	Conceives *The Spanish Gypsy*, beginning work on it as a drama; "Brother Jacob" is published in the *Cornhill*	Spencer, *Principles of Biology*; Newman, *Apologia pro Vita Sua*; Dickens, *Our Mutual Friend* (–1865); Gaskell, *Wives and Daughters* (–1866); Thackeray, *Denis Duval*; Trollope, *Can you Forgive Her?*
1865	Lewes accepts the editorship of the *Fortnightly Review*; he persuades her to drop work on her Spanish drama which has developed slowly; in March begins work on *Felix Holt, the Radical*	Assassination of President Lincoln; completion of the transatlantic cable; development of antiseptic surgery by Lister; Arnold, *Essays in Criticism*; Ruskin, *Sesame and Lilies*; Carroll, *Alice's Adventures in Wonderland*
1866	Corresponds with Frederic Harrison on legal details in *Felix Holt*, which is published in June. Resumes work on *The Spanish Gypsy*, converting it from drama to poem. Travels to France and Spain	Riots in Hyde Park; Aeronautical Society of Great Britain founded; Swinburne, *Poems and Ballads*; Trollope, *Last Chronicle of Barset* (–1867)
1867	Studies Spanish and reads more deeply in the philosophy of Comte; returns to London in March; in November discusses Emily Davies' proposal for a woman's college; at Blackwood's suggestion, writes an "Address to the Working Men" in the person of Felix Holt, as response to demands for political reform	Fenian agitation; Second Reform Bill passed; Dominion of Canada established; Arnold, *New Poems*; *Culture and Anarchy* (–1868); Carlyle, "Shooting Niagara: and After?"; Trollope, *Phineas Finn* (–1869); Marx, *Das Kapital* vol. I

1868	*Spanish Gypsy* finished in April; The Priory becomes a focus for intellectual discussion; visit from Darwin in November	Disraeli then Gladstone serves as Prime Minister; Browning, R., *The Ring and the Book* (–1869): Morris, *The Earthly Paradise* (–1870); Collins, *The Moonstone*
1869	Turns to the planning of *Middlemarch*; visits from D. G. Rossetti and Henry James; Lewes' son Thornton, gravely ill, returns to England; GE composes her "Brother and Sister" sonnets; pursues medical research for *Middlemarch*; Thornton dies in October; GE meets John Walter Cross who will become her second husband	Opening of the Suez Canal; Girton College, Cambridge founded; Mill, *On the Subjection of Women*; Lecky, *A History of European Morals*; Tennyson, *The Holy Grail and Other Poems*
1870	Finishes "The Legend of Jubal"; Lewes ill; the Franco-Prussian War upsets her deeply; allows Lewes to read the early chapters of *Middlemarch*; begins a work called "Miss Brooke" in November, and in December decides to join it to *Middlemarch*	Franco-Prussian War; death of Dickens; Dickens, *The Mystery of Edwin Drood*; Forster's Education Act; first Married Women's Property Act; Huxley, *Lay Sermons*; Newman, *Grammar of Assent*; Spencer, *Principles of Psychology*
1871	Works steadily on *Middlemarch* which begins to appear at the end of the year; visit from Turgenev; beginning of friendship with Tennyson, who reads "Maud" to GE and Lewes	Trade unions legalized; Religious tests abolished at Oxford and Cambridge; Stanley finds Livingstone at Ujiji; Darwin, *The Descent of Man*; Carroll, *Through the Looking-Glass*; Swinburne, *Songs Before Sunrise*
1872	Books II through VIII of *Middlemarch* appear at regular intervals through the year; summer at Redhill Surrey where she writes the last three books; intensely enthusiastic reception as the work appears; during visit to Homburg witnesses a gambling scene that inspires idea for *Daniel Deronda*	Voting by secret ballot established in Ballot Act; Butler, *Erewhon*; Hardy, *Under the Greenwood Tree*; *A Pair of Blue Eyes*

George Eliot's life and work	Historical and literary events
1873 Takes great pleasure from the rapturous response to *Middlemarch*; visits from Browning, Darwin, Emerson; reads *Tristram Shandy* and Aristotle's *Poetics*; studies works on Judaism for *Deronda*	Mill, *Autobiography*; Spencer, *The Study of Sociology*; Arnold, *Literature and Dogma*; Pater, *Studies in the History of the Renaissance*; Trollope, *Phineas Redux* (−1874)
1874 Struggles with *Deronda* in the early part of the year; has a first attack from a kidney stone; reads Trollope and Austen	First Impressionist exhibition in Paris; Disraeli becomes Prime Minister; Hardy, *Far from the Madding Crowd*; Thomson, *The City of Dreadful Night*
1875 Lewes publishes volume II of *Problems of Life and Mind* and *On Actors and Acting*; in May another bout of kidney distress; summer in Hertfordshire where she works on *Deronda*, and in October sends first two volumes to Blackwood	
1876 In February *Deronda* begins to appear in first of eight monthly intervals; novel sells very well, but GE is distressed at the critical response	Queen Victoria declared Empress of India; Alexander Graham Bell invents the telephone; Bradley, *Ethical Studies*; James, *Roderick Hudson*
1877 More kidney difficulty; third volume of Lewes' *Problems of Life and Mind* published; Richard and Cosima Wagner become regular acquaintances for a time	Russo-Turkish War; Edison invents phonograph; Mallock, *The New Republic*
1878 At the rate of one volume a month the Cabinet edition of her works appears; in June Lewes begins to suffer the effects of his cancer; GE writes *Theophrastus Such*; on 30 November Lewes dies.	Whistler versus Ruskin libel case; Hardy, *Return of the Native*; James, *The Europeans*; Swinburne, *Poems and Ballads*, second series

1879 Intense mourning for Lewes; enters almost complete isolation, then begins regular contact with Cross; takes pleasure in the reception of *Theophrastus Such*; works at completing the remaining volumes of Lewes' *Problems of Life and Mind*

Browning, R., *Dramatic Idyls*; Meredith, *The Egoist*; Trollope, *The Duke's Children*; Spencer, *Principles of Ethics*

1880 Gradually begins to see her friends again; Cross three times proposes marriage and is finally accepted in April; the wedding takes place on 6 May; her brother Isaac breaks his long silence in order to congratulate her; after a wedding trip through France, Germany and Italy, GE and Cross return to England and in December settle at 4 Cheyne Walk; on 19 December GE falls ill and dies three days later; buried alongside Lewes in Highgate Cemetery

Gladstone returns as Prime Minister; Disraeli, *Endymion*; Gissing, *Workers in the Dawn*

Summary of plot

On the eve of the great Reform Bill of 1832 and under the shadow of changes in every walk of life, the town of Middlemarch and its surrounding countryside become the site of diverse personal events that gradually resolve themselves into four chief narratives. The first is the story of Dorothea Brooke's moral and romantic awakening. The plot turns on her escape from the mistaken hopes she places in her first husband, the fussy cleric and pedantic scholar Edward Casaubon, and then, after Casaubon's death, on her surprised discovery that she loves his young cousin Will Ladislaw who, like Dorothea, is in search of life's proper vocation. The complicated relationship between public vocation and private emotion is what links this first plot to the plot of Tertius Lydgate and Rosamond Vincy. With the limitless ambition of a young doctor at a moment of great medical transition, Lydgate aims to professional success and gives only passing thought to the rest of life. Rosamond has little interest in medical ambition but consuming interest in the romance that she has projected onto her married life with Lydgate. The downward course of both the marriage and the medical career gives the book its darkest tones. On the other hand, the third love story in *Middlemarch*, which recounts the love between Rosamond's brother Fred and Mary Garth, is self-consciously idyllic. It is disturbed only in consoling ways when the Reverend Camden Farebrother appears as a worthy rival for Mary's affections. That a love dating from childhood can withstand such a challenge and can wind its way to a happy marriage allows it to stand as a pastoral counterpart to the stresses in the other two romance plots. The fourth main plot of the novel can scarcely be thought of as a romance narrative. It concerns the fall of Nicholas Bulstrode, a severely religious banker, whose moral grip on

Middlemarch is broken when he murders the blackmailing
John Raffles to keep him from revealing Bulstrode's un-
savory past. Although this plot follows a logic quite different
from the three marriage narratives, it interpenetrates with
them, and as with the other plots, it involves a large cast of
minor characters who would defeat any attempt at summary.

Chapter 1

The context of the novel

From rebel to sage

In the last years of the 1860s, when she began to conceive and then draft this monumental novel, George Eliot occupied a position of great eminence in English intellectual life. There is irony in her eminence. Two decades earlier, when she first left her home in the English Midlands and entered London intellectual circles, she had been a free-thinking, even subversive, radical who seemed destined to remain at odds with the dominant values of her society. Moreover, when in 1853 George Eliot decided to join her life to that of George Henry Lewes, she estranged many others who tolerated the free thinking but shuddered at the free living. Lewes, a versatile and well-known man of letters, had been unable to gain a divorce from his wife, and when his intellectual companionship with George Eliot grew into an emotional one, the two became the subject of widespread gossip and calumny. In both polite society and much of the artistic and intellectual community, George Eliot was deemed unfit to be received. All the more remarkable, then, that at the time of composing *Middlemarch* she had won a loyal and reverent audience which included the Queen of England, and had achieved the position of a moral sage, a position only confirmed and extended by the success of *Middlemarch*.

And yet, when she began to write the novel, she found herself in a condition of artistic uncertainty. For a long time, she was unsure of the subject of her novel; she was even unsure whether her next ambitious work would take the form of a novel. As it happened, her uncertainties turned out to be extremely fruitful. The great size of the imaginative *Middlemarch* owes much to the strains upon the imagination of its author, strains which pulled her in many directions and which obliged her to stretch the grasp of her novel. Two tendencies, in particular, reveal the conflicting pressures that underlay the conception of the project. The first is George Eliot's aspiration to what we may think of as the *universalist* vision, the grand encompassing panorama that would survey the history of European civilisation. The synoptic vision, which had long been an attraction to her, shows itself in the inclination to make a fictional world out of distant historical moments and to see in them the manifestation of some essential human aspiration and some fundamental conflict. The novel *Romola* (1863), which took as its subject the religious and political life of Renaissance Florence, epitomized George Eliot's interest in the large-scale historical synthesis – for instance, the synthesis of classical and Christian culture – as it stands illuminated at some turning-point in European history. Before beginning work on *Middlemarch*, George Eliot was contemplating a long poem about Timoleon, the Greek defender of freedom, which would have addressed the problem of the "influence of personal character on destinies." This is precisely the kind of highly general historical issue that frequently stirred her imagination.

Opposed to her universalism stands the second recurrent tendency in George Eliot's imaginative life, namely her regionalism, her abiding attraction to local experience, especially the local experience of the English Midlands where she passed her childhood. It has been said of George Eliot that the fundamental rhythm of her artistic life comprised a movement between the universalist and regionalist ambitions, but, however true this may be of her earlier work, it seems clear that in *Middlemarch* the two tendencies meet – not always comfortably. On the one hand, the novel preserves the synoptic ambition expressed in its opening sentence, the desire to study the "history of man" as it displays itself "under the varying experiments of Time." On the other hand, the book gives meticulous attention to the accidents and incidents of provincial life in nineteenth-century England.

To speak of "regionalism" in George Eliot's work is not only to speak of region in the spatial sense – a particular corner of the map of the world. It is also to speak in the temporal sense – a region of time, which in the case of *Middlemarch* spans a brief period from the late 1820s to the early 1830s. George Eliot trained herself to be one of those rare minds capable of surveying the length and breadth of human endeavour. Why then did her widely observing eye light on this piece of English soil at this season of its history?

Religion and science

Middlemarch is an historical novel that gives painstakingly detailed attention to events that had occurred forty years before its composition. Yet, consistently throughout the book, sometimes implicitly, sometimes explicitly, the historical narrative is haunted by the contemporary situation of England, the condition of the nation in the years 1868 to 1871. To talk about the context of the novel is inevitably to talk about two contexts: the context of the writing (George Eliot in 1869) and the context of the written (her characters in 1829); and it is necessarily to see the deep connections between these two moments in nineteenth-century life.

Two events of the 1860s absorbed the social attention of George Eliot and drew her universalizing mind toward the special concerns of a nation and a village. The first of these was the passage of the Second Reform Bill in 1867, which extended the suffrage to include most of the working men of England. Like others of her generation, George Eliot saw the bill as marking a decisive threshold in the social history of England, and in her case it directed her imagination back to the period of the First Reform Bill which was finally passed in 1832.

The sense of impending social change of uncertain magnitude greatly unsettled George Eliot, prompting her to reflect on the concept of reform not just in the political sense but in a more extended sense that included scientific, political, religious, and personal change. In *Middlemarch* itself the fates of Lydgate the doctor, Ladislaw the artistic dilettante, Middlemarch the community, and Dorothea Brooke the latter-day St. Theresa are all understood in terms of the opportunities and hazards of reform.

What makes this issue so charged in the case of George Eliot is that the provocations of reform became more than simply useful subject-matter for a new novel. They became the occasion for her to reconsider the movement of her own changing intellectual life. *Middlemarch* juxtaposes those two distinct moments – the passage of the First and Second Reform Bills, 1832 and 1867 – but it also recapitulates much of George Eliot's own history between those dates, a history of changing attitudes toward change itself.

As an adolescent in the 1830s George Eliot held to a strict form of Evangelical piety, a quality of faith so rigorous that it led her to extreme gestures of self-denial. When Dorothea Brooke, in the first chapter of *Middlemarch*, refuses to accept her dead mother's lovely jewels even as she feels the splendor of their beauty, and when she looks forward to giving up her horseback riding that she enjoys so passionately, she is an image of the young George Eliot who turned so firmly from the allure of the senses to the purity of the spirit. All the more remarkable, then, is George Eliot's movement from orthodox piety to religious radicalism. A sternly devout provincial young woman of twenty, by the age of thirty-five she had established herself as a significant presence in the radical intellectual life of London and had translated two of the most serious challenges to Victorian faith, David Friedrich Strauss's *Life of Jesus* (1846) and Ludwig Feuerbach's *The Essence of Christianity* (1854).

Of the two, the work of Feuerbach (1804–1872) is the more important to George Eliot's literary and intellectual development. Its great sceptical claim is that religion is a human construction which has prevented social progress by diverting reverence from humanity itself to the theological images it has made: "man in relation to God denies his own knowledge, his own thoughts, that he may place them in God." The urgent task, then, is to take back what has been surrendered to God, and so Feuerbach urges "the realization and humanization of God – the transformation and dissolution of theology into anthropology." Humanity, not divinity, must become the object of worship. In a bitterly caustic essay of 1855, "Evangelical Teaching: Dr. Cumming," George

Eliot accused the preacher John Cumming of a "perversion" of "true moral development" through his "substitution of a reference to the glory of God for the direct promptings of the sympathetic feelings." With Feuerbach she held that human capacities are the source of any divine promise, and in a letter she spoke of the fundamental belief that had allowed her to become a writer of fiction, "namely, that the fellowship between man and man which has been the principle of development, social and moral, is not dependent on conceptions of what is not man: and that the idea of God, so far as it has been a high spiritual influence, is the ideal of a goodness entirely human (i.e. an exaltation of the human)."

One of the main centers of moral value in *Middlemarch* is located in the Reverend Camden Farebrother who savors his pipe, enjoys his card-playing, and takes unabashed delight in the natural and human environment that surrounds him. Early in the work we learn that Farebrother realizes he is in the wrong profession, his devotion to the visible universe struggling against his obligation to serve an invisible God. Farebrother is an emblem of the great historical transition sketched out by Feuerbach; he is caught between a theological tradition and a modern anthropology; and his moral distinction for George Eliot resides in his ability to live as a theologian who worships the God in, not above, humanity and the natural world.

The liberation of humanity from a jealously oppressive theology, the creation of the "religion of humanity" — these are the animating ideals of George Eliot's early radicalism, and in the early 1850s the ideal was confirmed and strengthened through her encounter with the thought of Auguste Comte (1798–1853). Comte had elaborated a scheme of development according to which human history passes through three stages: the age of theology, the age of metaphysics, and the dawning age of positive science. In 1851 George Eliot described Comte's "positivist" belief that "theological and metaphysical speculation have reached their limit, and that the only hope of extending man's source of knowledge and happiness is to be found in positive science, and in the universal application of its principles." G. H. Lewes was one of Comte's earliest sympathetic readers in

England, and his keen enthusiasm for positivism would itself have been enough to rouse George Eliot's interest. But even apart from the strong influence of Lewes, George Eliot came into significant contact with other English Comteans, including Richard Congreve and Frederick Harrison, and although it would be a mistake to see her as a slavish follower of the positivist doctrine, it is essential to acknowledge that, like Feuerbach, Comte offered her certain fundamental intellectual insights that she studied, criticized, transformed, and then absorbed.

Certainly the most important recognition that she took from Comte was that after the theological age of faith in the supernatural and the miraculous, and after the metaphysical age of faith in forces, causes and essences, it was now possible to live fully in the age of science, which enjoins us not to look behind the veil of experience, but rather to give ourselves to a new revelation, the revelation stirred by the "patient watching of external fact":

The master key to this revelation, is the recognition of the presence of undeviating law in the material and moral world – of that invariability of sequence which is acknowledged to be the basis of physical science, but which is still perversely ignored in our social organization, our ethics and our religion. It is this invariability of sequence which can alone give value to experience and render education in the true sense possible.

("The Influence of Rationalism", 1865)

What she calls "the supreme unalterable nature of things" is the basis not only for a new science, but for a morality, and indeed for a new fiction.

The sharp contrast in *Middlemarch* between the dusty cleric Casaubon and the vibrant doctor Lydgate, and the associated contrast between the futile search for an obsolete truth and the fertile quest for a new truth, owe a great deal to George Eliot's reading of Comte. As James Scott has persuasively shown, Casaubon is the emblem of Comte's Metaphysical Man, committed to discovering secret origins and forces, while Lydgate is a figure for the new positive scientist, who will work through "careful observation and inference." Both are ambitious questers – Casaubon pursuing the Key to All

Mythologies, and Lydgate in search of the "primary tissue" in human biology. Neither is in a position to reach the ultimate ground, the deep foundation. But as Will Ladislaw disdainfully observes, Casaubon's ignorance of the new German biblical criticism, work of the sort translated by George Eliot, makes his project obsolete before he begins; Casaubon has not understood that the study of mythology, like the study of chemistry, is a science in constant change. On the other hand, Lydgate has grasped the principle of positive inquiry that his fellow physicians archaically deny and that lets him gesture toward the future of medical science.

Yet, Lydgate's failure is as thorough as Casaubon's, a fact that has always troubled readers of *Middlemarch* who have wanted to see in the energetic young physician a figure of modern heroism. George Eliot's refusal to allow Lydgate the heroic outcome is no idle perversity. It is a refusal tightly connected to other commitments that make George Eliot such a complex thinker and *Middlemarch* such an intricate book.

The powers of the past

If there is a single leading cause of Lydgate's failure, it is his inability to acknowledge and to embrace the past. He carelessly discards his aristocratic pedigree, and in denying his family history, he not only antagonizes relations who might help him in his financial need; but he also fatally misunderstands the attraction he holds for his wife Rosamond. Still more seriously, Lydgate disowns his romantic history, which provides the most melodramatic episode in the book. The young doctor's infatuation with the actress Laure; his sudden uncontrollable declaration of love; his shock when he learns that she has intentionally killed her first husband — all these Lydgate dismisses as isolated moments of self-abandonment that are unrepeatable and therefore unthreatening. The narrator of *Middlemarch*, however, heavily underscores Lydgate's inability to escape the precedent of his trying affair with Laure. When he abruptly proposes marriage to Rosamond, despite all his resolves to place his profession well before his family, Lydgate enacts George Eliot's version of

Marx's dictum, that those who ignore the past are condemned to repeat it.

The supreme value of the past is the countervailing pressure to George Eliot's radicalism. It is what separates her from the liberationist rhetoric found in Feuerbach and Comte, and also what injects ambiguity and dissonance into her vision of social change and political hope. As she put it in 1851, Comte's notion of a triumphant progress from theology to metaphysics to positive science gives only one aspect of the cultural wholeness we must seek, the other aspect being a generous retrospective glance on the history of culture. "Every past phase of human development," she writes, "is part of that education of the race in which we are sharing; every mistake, every absurdity into which poor human nature has fallen, may be looked on as an experiment of which we may reap the benefit" ("The Progress of the Intellect," 1851). There can be no question then of smashing the idols of past superstition. Those idols were products of the same yearnings, the same hopes, that animate the nineteenth century.

The rise of science, argued G. H. Lewes, has left the modern mind with two choices: to extinguish religion or to transform it. George Eliot, like Lewes, chose transformation over extinction; and transformation meant that, while the supernatural canopy of divine miracle would be abandoned, the persistent human impulse toward faith and reverence would remain – only now, it would be a reverence, not for an unseen God, but for the visible humanity which has developed the idea and the image of God. For George Eliot this implies an abiding respect for religions of the past, because "all the great religions of the world historically considered, are rightly the objects of deep reverence and sympathy – they are the record of spiritual struggles which are types of our own." Tradition, then, is not a constraint; it is both the source of the present and the mirror of its difficulties; and the radical in this view is the one who plans for the future by studying the past.

The political implications of this attitude had begun to manifest themselves in *Felix Holt, the Radical*, published in 1866, and after the passage of the Second Reform Bill in

1867, George Eliot's publisher John Blackwood suggested that she deliver some urgent advice to the working men who now, through the extension of the vote, stood to gain such power. The "Address to the Working Men, by Felix Holt" appeared early in 1868, and it contains reflections on the problem of reform that are highly pertinent to an understanding of *Middlemarch*.

"I expect great changes," announces Felix, "and I desire them. But I don't expect them to come in a hurry." He expects them rather in their due time. Here is the metaphor that guides George Eliot's reflections on reform, the metaphor of moral maturity, of political ripeness — most generally the metaphor of society as a vital organism obeying its own laws of growth and decline. The prosperity and well being of England, says the fictional Felix to the real workers, is a "vast crop, that like the corn in Egypt can be come at, not at all by hurried snatching, but only by a well-judged patient process." And in another strategically motivated image, Felix suggests that "society stands before us like that wonderful piece of life, the human body, with all its various parts depending on one another, and with a terrible liability to get wrong because of that delicate dependence."

George Eliot's impersonation of the eloquent artisan Felix Holt gave great pleasure to her cautious publisher Blackwood, but it is doubtful whether it gave much delight to those newly enfranchised workers who were eager to test the powers of reform. Her organicist social theory emphasized not rights but duties; it celebrated not freedom but renunciation, renunciation for the sake of that vital body, the community, that alone gave life to the various parts. The working class may be one strong limb of that body, a limb now strong enough to kick, but in Felix Holt's vision the task for the working class is to learn not how to kick but how to walk, carrying the interdependent body where it wants to go.

There is no need to doubt George Eliot's acceptance of radical change, but it is to be a slow radicalism, slow enough to avoid battering down the monuments of the past. So Felix Holt cautions the workers against giving a "fatal shock" to the "living body" of society; he warns against tampering with the existing system of class distinctions; he insists that "we have to submit ourselves to the great law of inheritance." For George Eliot the greatness of that law lies in what she calls "the common estate of society," by which she means chiefly the *cultural* acquisitions from the past: "that treasure of knowledge, science, poetry, refinement of thought, feeling and manners, great memories and the interpretation of great records, which is carried on from the minds of one generation to another." The thought that the emancipated workers might trample on the great books, soiling them beyond recovery – this is the spectre that haunts George Eliot. It is what leads her to make *education* the center of her reformist program, inspired by the thought that when the working class can be educated in the beauties of art and science, it will make its radical reforms with care and patience, stepping carefully around the flowers of the past.

The Woman Question

One of those flowers of the past is called Woman. Even more than she felt the provocation of the advancing working class, George Eliot felt, and suffered from, the provocation of the Woman Question. This is the other great question of the late 1860s that obliged her to confront the issue of reform. The drive for extension of the suffrage to women, the movement to found a woman's college, the general and contentious question of separate spheres for men and women – there was no ignoring such concerns, especially for a woman such as George Eliot whose own life seemed such a sharp challenge to the conventions of gender.

After her high-minded attack on "evangelical teaching" was printed in the *Westminster Review*, George Eliot wrote to Charles Bray asking him to keep the sex of the author a secret. "The article," she notes, "appears to have produced a strong impression, and that impression would be a little counteracted if the author were known to be a *woman*." The *anonymity* of her early essays and the *pseudonymity* of her novels are both signs of her attempt to break free from the

Victorian "laws" of gender, to speak and write beyond the terms of a sexual distinction that deprived women's writing and the reception of that writing of their intellectual force.

Yet, if she aimed for an impersonal authority, disguised by the name of a man, the episodes of her life and the events of her time made it impossible for her to forget the special burdens of being a woman. The opprobrium that attached to her relationship with Lewes and the general agitation over the rights and responsibilities of women forced her to meet an issue she often preferred to avoid. During the early stages of *Middlemarch* she confided to a correspondent that "There is no subject on which I am more inclined to hold my peace and learn, than on the 'Women Question.' It seems to me to overhang abysses, of which even prostitution is not the worst." Then she goes on to say: "do not let any one else see this note. I have been made rather miserable lately by revelations about women, and have resolved to remain silent in my sense of helplessness. I know very little about what is specially good for women – only a few things that I feel sure are good for human nature generally" (4 Oct 1869).

Middlemarch itself is a long, long testimony to her *inability* to hold her peace, her need to discover a form of speech suitable to the Woman Question. Yet, her hesitation is not surprising. On one side stands her resolute traditionalism, her desire to preserve ancestral forms of life that belong to the organic history of our species. On the other side stands the glaring example of her own life, her sharp uncompromising break with the conventions of marriage, her refusal to submit to oppressive customs. Her very success as a moral sage made clear that the rude dismissals of woman's intellectual insufficiency were inadequate. Yet her own example was not enough to persuade her that the ideology of "separate spheres" was obsolete. In an 1868 letter to Emily Davies, one of the most active supporters of the feminist cause, George Eliot praised the "spiritual wealth" that was a product of the "physiological differences between women and men," and she spoke of the need to preserve gentleness and tenderness as the distinctive emotional province of women. Notoriously, she refused to support John Stuart Mill's attempt to extend the vote to women, speaking of the suffrage as "an extremely doubtful good."

Still, all this is not to imply that George Eliot capitulated to the prevailing devaluations of women's talent. It is rather to suggest the fearful impasse of her social and cultural position, the position of a woman artist leading a revolutionary life while enshrining the virtues of tradition. The revealing essay of 1856, "Silly Novels by Lady Novelists," which was written just before she began her career as a writer of fiction, well expresses the acute difficulties of writing as a woman in the middle of the nineteenth century. Most of the essay − and it is important to remember that it too was presented from the more secure vantage point of anonymity − is an attack on the "composite order of feminine fatuity" in novel writing, a mixed product of "the frothy, the prosy, the pious, or the pedantic." It becomes difficult to resist the implication that the two halves of the essay's title are more than contingently related, that George Eliot means us to see silliness as the particular domain of lady novelists. But then in the last pages of the essay she works to resist that implication. Thinking no doubt of Austen and the Brontës, she recalls the remarkable success of past female writers. In a characteristic maneuver she opposes the vulgarity of the present with the dignity of the past, a dignity expressed in the recognition by great women novelists of their "precious speciality, lying quite apart from masculine aptitudes and experience." It is a celebrated phrase, and one helpful way to think about *Middlemarch* is to see it as an extended and rigorous meditation on the speciality of women. What is that precious speciality? How may it prosper?

Rosamond Vincy, the prize pupil of Mrs. Lemon's finishing school, is offered as an epitome of what nineteenth-century society seeks in its women: "a rare compound of beauty, cleverness, and amiability" (III, 27). As the novel insistently reminds us, Rosamond is a social achievement, a cultural construction, a product of refined artifice; at Mrs. Lemon's school "the teaching included all that was demanded in the accomplished female − even to extras, such as the getting

in and out of a carriage'' (I, 11). It is the assumption of
Lydgate, and the sexual ideology surrounding him, that Rosamond's "perfect womanhood" is essentially that of a docile,
pliable, submissive being, "an accomplished creature who
venerated his high musings and momentous labours and
would never interfere with them" (IV, 36). The great turn in
their marriage, and the crucial turn in George Eliot's attack
on modern femininity, is that Rosamond proves to be, not the
mild wife submitting to the husband's greater power, but the
worthy antagonist with unsuspected powers of her own. For
George Eliot – in what is perhaps the most disturbing of her
conclusions on the subject of gender – the great problem
posed by the Woman Question was not the indignity suffered
by women who must surrender their strength to men; it was
rather the cruelty and moral violence concealed beneath the
myth of submission, leading the "accomplished female" to
become the mirror image of the powerful male. With horror
Lydgate comes to realize that "his will was not a whit
stronger than hers" and that "As to saying that he was
master, it was not the fact" (VII, 64). And when he
understands the irretrievable failure of their marriage, we
read that "He wished to excuse everything in her if he could
– but it was inevitable that in that excusing mood he should
think of her as if she were an animal of another and feebler
species. Nevertheless she had mastered him" (VII, 65).

The reference to the animal species in this climactic passage is
too conspicuous to ignore. It points us to one further element in
the intellectual context of *Middlemarch*, namely the looming
influence of Darwin's *Origin of Species*, published in 1859.
Studying the book with the greatest attention, George Eliot
read it alongside Lewes whose own work in biology let him
be a useful guide to Darwin's technicalities. In 1868, with
Middlemarch on the verge of conception, Lewes published a
series of articles on Darwin in the *Fortnightly Review*, which,
as Gillian Beer has persuasively argued, were the discursive
source of George Eliot's imaginative appropriation of Darwin's
ideas. Beer points out that no notion has greater pertinence
to the workings of *Middlemarch* than Darwin's recognition
that individuals can always escape from the types and classes

we construct for them. Our notions of species represent our attempt to tame and fix the rich variety of nature. Or, in Lewes' words, "Species, except as a subjective classification of resemblances, has no existence. Only individuals with variable resemblances exist;" and in this thought about the taxonomy of species, George Eliot found her way back to the question of woman.

The "Prelude" to *Middlemarch*, having invoked the epic grandeur of Saint Theresa, turns to the failures of those women who have aspired to grandeur and who have failed.

Some have felt that these blundering lives are due to the inconvenient indefiniteness with which the Supreme Power has fashioned the natures of women: if there were one level of feminine incompetence as strict as the ability to count three and no more, the social lot of women might be treated with scientific certitude. Meanwhile the indefiniteness remains, and the limits of variation are really much wider than any one would imagine from the sameness of women's coiffure and the favourite love-stories in prose and verse.

Here is George Eliot's Darwinian feminism: a refusal to accept Woman as a fixed essence. When Lydgate first meets Rosamond Vincy he thinks, "That is what a woman ought to be" (I, 11), and he rejoices in her "distinctive womanhood." This is one way of classifying the species – as "polished, refined, docile" (II, 16); later, when he begins to class Rosamond as the "animal of another and feebler species," he has radically changed his definition of the species. But in both instances, the telling move is Lydgate's impulse to generalize and to determine the essential character of femininity.

Of Dorothea, Lydgate initially feels that she "did not look at things from the proper feminine angle" (I, 11). From the standpoint of the usual sexual conventions, Dorothea appears as a sport of nature, an oddity, even a freak. But by the end of the novel Lydgate's faint distaste will turn into the reverent perception that "She seems to have what I never saw in any woman before"(VIII, 76). Through the gloriously opposing instance of Dorothea, *Middlemarch* offers a vehement repudiation of the species "Woman," as nineteenth-century England had come to construct her. And yet in her critique of the politics of gender, George Eliot could not follow her feminist friends, could not call for the invention of new worlds for women that would break decisively with the old. This is in part because she could not accept Lewes' sharp distinction between the species and the individual, and so could not imagine progress merely through the liberation of particular individuals, especially women, from the false constraints of species. In the exacting spirit of her radical traditionalism, she wanted to escape the pernicious construction of a feminine species, not by reaching toward an unconstrained future, but by recovering certain productive constraints of the past. It is not that Dorothea is an unprecedented individual who cannot be sorted according to any classification; it is that *different* classes are required. So, in the opening description in the "Prelude," she is linked to the "cygnet [who] is reared uneasily among the ducklings in the brown pond, and never finds the living stream in fellowship with its own oary-footed kind." Hers is not the common kind; but it is a kind nonetheless, the kind, for instance, of those many Theresas who have lived since their Spanish original. Yet, in good Darwinian fashion, George Eliot sees Dorothea not merely as the latest, the most up-to-date, example of the fixed Theresan essence, but as the representative of a species transformed by her encounters with a changing environment. Dorothea Brooke, obliged to live outside a time and place in which she might flourish, obliged rather to live in the unpropitious circumstances of the early nineteenth century, can be neither simply a member of her noble kind, nor simply an individual. She is a hybrid, whose suffering and whose greatness derive from the fact that human beings cannot surrender themselves to their eternal essences but must live and change in history.

1830 and the novel as history

Because there survive a large number of notebook jottings made during the writing of *Middlemarch*, it is possible to get a firm sense of what it meant to George Eliot to situate her novel in history. She was a tireless researcher who saw reading as a great stimulus to writing. But what most stands out in any consideration of the *Middlemarch* notebooks is the range of her reading and the diversity of her interests. Law, medicine, poetry, astronomy, philology, politics – she gave careful attention to all of these subjects, dutifully copying quotations and noting facts. Indeed the notebooks are predominantly books of Fact, inspired by George Eliot's robust sense of material existence, her evident delight in the contingent details of worldly life for their own sake. So amidst the notes on striking events in the history of Europe, she suddenly records without context the fact that "Some mushrooms yield 60,000 spores in a minute." The delight in the actual, no matter how mean and humble the actuality, is essential to her sense of the life of human beings within historical time.

The constellation of particular facts that surround and penetrate particular lives tends to be identified in George Eliot's writing by the term "condition," a word that seems to convey to her a sense of the inevitable *circumstantiality* of living – the recognition, as she put it in *Felix Holt*, that "there is no private life which has not been determined by a wider public life." In an essay of the mid-1860s she suggests that if superstition has waned in recent centuries, it is not because the multitude of human beings have developed stronger inward capacities of reason, but because of what she calls "external Reason – the sum of conditions resulting from the laws of material growth." Among those conditions are "the increase of population, the rejection of convicts by our colonies, [and] the exhaustion of the soil by cotton plantations." The pressures of circumstance have roused people out of their irrational superstition, and while "external Reason" does not predetermine our inner lives, it is for George Eliot the medium in which we move, the medium which colors our sensations and our emotions, and which we ignore at our great peril.

Once George Eliot had settled on provincial life during the period of the First Reform Bill as the historical site of her ambitious novel, she undertook to articulate the specific "conditions" of life at this apparent threshold to modernity. Her intention was not to establish some hierarchy of social pressures but to record the diversity of circumstances impinging on individual destinies, and also the destiny of small social groups. She investigated the spread of cholera through Europe in the early 1830s; she noted the coming of the railroads to the English countryside; she recorded small details of provincial taste in clothes, in slang, in poetry; she incorporated references to the new biblical criticism that had so deeply affected her own provincial experience; and in countless ways she set out to evoke the habits and customs of this particular place at this particular time.

In her studied, even relentless, effort to recreate the web of conditions characterizing an historical moment, George Eliot gave special attention to two large areas of concern, both well represented in her surviving notebook entries. The first is the rise of medical science which she studied carefully in various histories of medicine and in the pages of the medical journal, *The Lancet*. It is not surprising that this subject should have interested her so greatly. Given her strong commitments to the emancipation of reason from superstition, and her Comtean perception that theology and metaphysics must give way to positive research, she naturally found the case of medicine in the early nineteenth century to be highly suggestive. On the one side, there was the exhilarating movement from pernicious fakery to modern science. Here the late eighteenth-century French physiologist Bichat occupied a special place. For George Eliot, and equally for Lydgate, Bichat stands as the harbinger of a new rigorous science that should give strong foundations to the archaic structure of medical practice: "the conception wrought out by Bichat" (thinks Lydgate), "with his detailed study of the different tissues, acted necessarily on medical questions as the turning of a gaslight would act on a dim, oil-lit street, showing new connections and hitherto hidden facts of structure which must be taken into account in considering the symptoms of maladies and the action of medicaments" (II, 15). But Lydgate immediately goes on to reflect that "now at the end of 1829, most medical practice was still strutting or shambling along the old paths," and this gives the other side of George Eliot's interest in medicine: namely, the obstacles in the way of enlightened science. Much of her research and much of the detail in *Middlemarch* is concerned not with scientific insights but with the structure of medical institutions which often directly oppose the interests of science. The powerful role of medical societies, the distorted requirements in the training of physicians, the jealous guarding of established interests, the difficulties in financing new hospitals – these issues occupy George Eliot as much as the distinction between typhus and typhoid (important in the recovery of Fred Vincy) or the newer treatments for delirium tremens (crucial in the death of Raffles). Lydgate's ultimate failure to achieve any of his scientific ambitions displays George Eliot's unsentimental view of the social and psychological powers that threaten to disarm rational inquiry.

The second significant historical focus is the realm of politics itself, specifically the agitation over the First Reform Bill as it worked its difficult way through Parliament. In her notebooks George Eliot carefully records the important dates in the passage of the bill – from its first motion (November 1830), to the dissolution of Parliament (April 1831), to the opposition of the House of Lords, to the reintroduction of the bill, to its final passage (June 1832), to the election of the Reformed Parliament (January 1833) – and at the same time she meticulously dates major events in the lives of her characters – marriage, death, birth – to correspond to these political episodes. Jerome Beaty has shown how thoroughly and yet unobtrusively *Middlemarch* maintains constant reference to the political struggles of the day. Characters go about their personal business; and the great events of the epoch, such as, for instance, the death of King George IV, impinge on their lives; but those events are referred to only in passing and only from within the context of customary provincial affairs.

The result is a complicated intersection between private and public life. As Beaty has observed, when Mr. Brooke comes to announce Dorothea's engagement to Will, both the characters and the reader are more interested in the news of the impending marriage than the momentous historical event, the dissolution of Parliament, which coincides with it. This is not only, as Beaty says, an example of how fiction

thrusts back an obtrusive history; it is also a telling instance
of how local concerns begin to attain a significance greater
than the large-scale political gestures which initially seem so
momentous.

During the first years of the 1870s the Franco-Prussian war
was following its violent course, much to the despair of the
author of *Middlemarch*. George Eliot, who had originally inclined to the side of the Germans, came to brood miserably
over the endless barbarism. In a letter of late 1870 she wrote
of her need to withdraw from the sordid social reality:

One has to dwell continually on the permanent, growing influence
of ideas, in spite of temporary reactions however violent, in order
to get courage and perseverance for any work which lies aloof from
the immediate wants of society. You remember Goethe's contempt
for the Revolution of '30, compared with the researches on the
Vertebrate Structure of the skull?

This remark has a useful bearing on the complicated
historical attitudes of *Middlemarch*, demonstrating as it does
George Eliot's suspicion of those political and military struggles that seem − but only seem − to direct the course of
history. By making the politics of reform so marginal to its
narrative, the novel suggests the decisive importance of a non-
political or, in the case of Caleb Garth, even an *anti-political*
mode of existence. One recurrent source of uneasiness among
readers has been the final restriction of Dorothea to private
morality, while Will enjoys the prerogatives available to an
"ardent public man." But given the marked scepticism
toward the political process, both in *Middlemarch* and in
George Eliot's non-fictional writings, the attractions of a
political life must appear sharply qualified.

Here a more speculative idea might be pertinent. In outlining
the bare bones of the plot, George Eliot described the dealings
between Bulstrode and the blackmailing Raffles and concludes this brief section of her notebook by adding the
somewhat surprising detail − surprising given how general
the other notes are here − that "Raffles comes back the third
time" to harass Bulstrode. What makes this so teasing to interpretation is that in giving a similar catalogue of political
dates, she had specifically referred to the introduction of the

Reform Bill for the third time. There can be no question of identifying the unregenerate Raffles with the spirit of reform; the analogy rather suggests the *discontinuity* between political and private history; and yet it also manages to suggest that the provocation of reform to the ruling classes is as disruptive, psychologically and morally, as Raffles' repeated insurgence against the powerful Bulstrode.

The issue is still more complicated, because the class basis of the struggle between Bulstrode and Raffles is a tension between middle-class banker and neglected laborer, while the First Reform Bill was a victory of the middle classes over the landed gentry. And yet, the *Second* Reform Bill, passed just before George Eliot began writing *Middlemarch*, took precisely the form of a conflict between the middle and the working class. The particular example points to a highly general problem in the representation of history in the novel; namely the ambiguous relations between the time of the fictional events (1827–1832) and the time of the writing itself (1869–1872). The extraordinary care taken to identify the particular circumstances of provincial life at the end of the 1820s works to distinguish the pre-Reform period of the narrative from the post-Reform period of the narrating. The characters in the fiction live in a time when science stumbled before the power of superstition, when medicine was dominated by quackery, when the railroads were seen as a monstrous intrusion into the countryside that might still be repulsed, when attitudes toward women were still unreconstructed. All this invites the reader to enjoy a comfortable superiority toward those living in a charming but benighted time. And yet as the Raffles–Bulstrode relation suggests, and as the novel implies in many other ways, a period that seemed to be a window onto the past reveals itself as a mirror of the present. In the late 1860s much of the Victorian middle class dreaded the power of the working class, as Bulstrode dreads the power of Raffles.

Insofar as the present tense of 1871 has freed itself from some of the needless cruelties and stupidities of almost half a century earlier – and the novel indeed suggests that to an extent this has occurred – then a benignly tolerant optimism can mitigate the sense of failure that so often colors the events. A latter-day Lydgate would not need to struggle so hopelessly against professional intransigence; a latter-day Farebrother might not miss his secular vocation. On the other hand, insofar as 1830 and 1870 are linked in their sense of modern bewilderment; insofar as the distinction between pre- and post-Reform fades next to the distinction between the old world of consoling faith evoked in the "Prelude," the world of St. Theresa, and the world of a sceptical modernity felt in 1830 as in 1870; insofar as the late nineteenth century has not resolved the problems of the early nineteenth century, then the novel moves from optimism toward tragedy. George Eliot is too complex and too tough-minded a thinker to choose between these alternatives. The test for her characters, and for her readers, is how to sustain the historical ambiguity and how to learn to live in it with grandeur.

Chapter 2

The method of *Middlemarch*

The discipline of the real

It is impossible to consider the history of realism in the novel, at least as that history passes through the English novel, without quickly naming *Middlemarch* as a landmark. In many respects it serves as the standard metre stick of the realist movement in fiction: George Levine has plausibly called it "the summa of Victorian realism." To the impatient question, But what do you *mean* by realism?, it is tempting just to lift the novel high and to say, I mean This. And yet if *Middlemarch* is a work which confirms and dignifies a central literary tradition, it is also a work which shows the unsteadiness, even the self-contradictions, of the realist project. George Eliot can be usefully seen as that English novelist who most forcefully expresses the claims of realism and who most vividly shows its instability.

The craving for detail so evident in her researches for the novel, in the desire to reproduce the bumpy textures of actuality, and in the eagerness to record the sheer contingent fact that mushrooms can yield 60,000 spores in a minute – all this is a product of that root realist yearning to surrender to the world as it is, to that "supreme unalterable nature of things." Some of the most celebrated passages in George Eliot's writing address the dignity and the urgency of the artist's engagement with ordinary life in all its homely familiarity.

"Paint us an angel, if you can," she writes in *Adam Bede*,

with a floating violet robe, and a face paled by the celestial light; paint us yet oftener a Madonna, turning her mild face upward and opening her arms to welcome the divine glory; but do not impose on us any aesthetic rules which shall banish from the region of Art those women scraping carrots with their work-worn hands, those heavy clowns taking holiday in a dingy pot-house, those rounded backs and stupid weather-beaten faces that have bent over the spade and done the rough work of the world – those homes with their tin pans, their brown pitchers, their rough curs, and their clusters of onions. In this world there are so many of these common coarse people, who have no picturesque sentimental wretchedness! It is so needful we should remember their existence, else we may happen to leave them quite out of our religion and philosophy, and frame lofty theories which only fit a world of extremes. Therefore let Art always remind us of them; therefore let us always have men ready to give the loving pains of a life to the faithful representing of commonplace things.

(II, 17)

This passage may be taken as the manifesto of that mid-Victorian realism that culminates in the novels of George Eliot and that takes as its credo "the faithful representing of commonplace things." It is clear that *Middlemarch* upholds this great realist commitment, upholds it particularly in its refusal to idealize its most attractive characters. Lydgate's "spots of commonness" (II, 15), Farebrother's weakness for card-playing, Dorothea's "fanaticism of sympathy" (II, 22), are telling examples of George Eliot's insistence on the streaks of impurity that run even through high moral character. The mixed conditions of ordinary experience give her the dramatic arena, in which characters must struggle toward a better life with only the usual instruments of the uncertain human will.

In this desire to purify art of its sentimental temptations, George Eliot participates in that broad movement of realism that saw itself as making a revolution in culture. Kant's great slogan of Enlightenment, "*Sapere aude*" (Dare to Know), epitomizes the realist desire to banish illusion and to leave an unadorned world open to inspection. "I cannot paint an angel," wrote the painter Gustave Courbet, "because I have never seen one." Here is the motto of realism, the affirmation of the real, the concrete, the perceptible. "The art of painting," held Courbet, "can only consist in the representation of objects visible and tangible for the artist." The paraphernalia of the pre-realist tradition – mythological scenes, saintly personages, figures of allegory – are to be smashed by the power of the Actual.

Painting offered one compelling model to the realist novelist, and it is clear that George Eliot's sensibility was nurtured by the example of the Dutch realists. In a characteristic description in *Middlemarch* the narrator sketches Mary Garth as an "ordinary sinner" — "she was brown; her curly dark hair was rough and stubborn; her stature was low" — and then goes on to say that "Rembrandt would have painted her with pleasure" (I, 12). And yet for all of George Eliot's devotion to Rembrandt, it is clear that the form of the novel posed difficulties and offered opportunities not present in the medium of paint.

In the 1842 preface to his extravagantly ambitious work *The Human Comedy*, Honoré de Balzac described his intention to record the "two or three thousand conspicuous types" of his period. "My work," he proclaimed, "has its geography, as it has its genealogy and its families, its places and things, its persons and their deeds; as it has its heraldry, its nobles and commonalty, its artisans and peasants, its politicians and dandies, its army — in short, a whole world of its own." This is where novelistic realism departs from realist painting, in this aspiration to become a *global* realism which can offer not only truth, but more supremely, the whole truth. George Eliot clearly shares this aspiration with Balzac. J. Hillis Miller has persuasively argued that *Middlemarch* aims toward a total picture of modern society. Although its subtitle is the seemingly more modest "A Study of Provincial Life," it is evident that George Eliot wants to record all the diverse conditions, all the varying pressures, of the given historical moment, and she seems guided by the notion that anything short of a total representation would distort the realist project. The huge cast of characters, the widely varying social contexts, the attention to theology, politics, science, fashion, the great range of hopes, fears, visions, terrors — all this is plainly part of the effort to evoke totality.

On the one hand, the realist abandons the large cast of airy personages who had dominated the cultural imagination. On the other hand, having surrendered the vast realm of the angels, the realist is left with — everything. This is the double force of the movement: an act of exclusion that is meant to restore the world to its proper wholeness. In place of the false vastness of superstition and fantasy, it offers the true magnitude of the ordinary world. The thin exotic realm evaporates, leaving behind the rich density of common life.

In his still unsurpassed work on the "representation of reality," *Mimesis* (1946), Erich Auerbach has given characterizations of the nineteenth-century realist movement that have an important bearing on *Middlemarch*. For Auerbach the first decisive step was to place human experience inside a concrete social context, or as he puts it,

He who would account to himself for his real life and his place in human society is obliged to do so upon a far wider practical foundation and in a far larger context than before, and to be continually conscious that the social base upon which he lives is not constant for a moment but is perpetually changing through convulsions of the most various kinds.

The French Revolution and its aftermath, the suddenly more rapid tempo of social change, the acute consciousness of social convulsion — in Auerbach's account, these historical forces created a new awareness that we live in the context of changing reality, and as a result "the serious realism of modern times cannot represent man otherwise than as embodded in a total reality, political, social, and economic, which is concrete and constantly evolving." For the first generation of realists, for Stendhal and Balzac, the commitment to the representation of concrete contemporary existence is accompanied by an often extravagant moral stridency. The description of modern life generates a passionate evaluation, often a denunciation, that expresses the judgments of an author deeply involved in the world he chronicles. But in the work of a second generation, argues Auerbach, especially in the work of Flaubert, a striking development occurs. The voice of judgment, the bombastic voice of denunciation or celebration, falls silent. For Flaubert the realist labor was to be "impartial," "impersonal," and "objective." The author withdraws from the representation: "An artist should be in his work like God in creation, invisible and all-powerful; he should be everywhere felt, but nowhere seen." A corollary is that "Art must rise above personal emotions and nervous susceptibilities. It is time to endow it with pitiless method, with the exactness of the physical sciences." Not involvement but detachment becomes the watchword of the realist artist.

Against the background of this account, the career of George Eliot assumes an interesting shape. With all the conviction of Flaubert, she felt that science was indispensable to a genuinely contemporary fiction. The precision of scientific method, the rigorous honesty of its look at the world, the unshrinking encounter with even ugly facts – these were high virtues for both writers. And yet, for George Eliot the temper of science presupposed no detachment, no withdrawal into impersonality. On the contrary, science generated sympathy; honesty yielded solidarity; in opening the world to direct inspection, scientific realism allowed for a form of understanding that would connect us to one another. Flaubert can write that "Between the crowd and ourselves no bond exists," but for George Eliot no justification for art is more fundamental than the creation of better social bonds. Science and morality are complementary human projects, and indeed the conjunction of science and morals is one of the most distinctive aspects of the method of *Middlemarch*.

Another contemporaneous turn in the novel, a turn that might be variously associated with Dickens and Dostoevsky, adds another strand to the context surrounding the fiction of George Eliot. Both Dickens and Dostoevsky were preoccupied with the nature of fictional realism; both often sought to justify their work in terms of its fidelity to the real; and yet both expressed disdain for the usual definitions of realism. Dostoevsky wrote that "What most regard as fantastic and lacking in universality, *I* hold to be the inmost essence of truth. And observation of everyday trivialities I have long ceased to regard as realism – it is quite the reverse." Dickens, for his part, saw his proper sphere as the "romantic side of familiar things." For both writers the way to reach the real was to surpass the merely familiar, to heighten, to exaggerate, to deform, to caricature, all in order to illuminate the reality veiled by everyday experience. The cult of science was a favorite target of Dickens and Dostoevsky, who saw scientific objectivity and impersonality as an obstacle to a perception of the inner truth.

Much of the method of George Eliot can be understood as a reversal of Dickens's slogan, "the romantic side of familiar things." The goal of her narrative realism is often to demonstrate the familiar side of romantic things, to show how those exotic possibilities which we contemplate in idle fantasy depend on ordinary, matter-of-fact desires, motives, and dispositions. Merely to set Raskolnikov's murder of two women against Bulstrode's murder of Raffles is to feel all the force of the difference. Dostoevsky follows the erratic movement of a personality wandering away from convention and habit into moral pathology, and it is from the standpoint of the grotesque that *Crime and Punishment* offers its reflections on the common fate of the soul. But it is one of the self-conscious responsibilities of *Middlemarch* to show how there is nothing grotesque about Bulstrode's slow descent toward murder. The extremity of a murder is dissolved into a myriad of familiar vacillations, ordinary fears, and everyday compromises. Part of the earnest teaching of *Middlemarch* is that what we call romance is merely the gradual unfolding of common realities.

It is possible, without undue simplification, to see George Eliot as marking out a *via media* between her most eminent contemporaries in the novel. She shared with Flaubert a conviction that scientific clarity would help to reform the novel, but she refused to follow science into the perfect detachment of impersonality. She joined with Dickens and Dostoevsky in her belief that a profound moral purpose was the justification of fiction, but she resisted the claim that profundity lay outside the usual boundaries of daily life. Science in her view did not deplete but nourished the moral sense; moral insight did not transcend the ordinary; it rested securely within it.

"Prosaic" might be a fit word for George Eliot's temperament as a novelist, not in any invidious sense, but in a positive double sense: first, to suggest her deliberate acceptance of unadorned daily life as the foundation of the novel; and second, to suggest her commitment to prose as a verbal medium. When Will Ladislaw becomes impatient to talk to Dorothea alone, the narrator compares modern love to the love of Dante and Beatrice, and Petrarch and Laura, wryly commenting that "in later days it is preferable to have fewer sonnets and more conversation" (IV, 37). The irony aside, it can be fairly

said that George Eliot's own preferences lie more to prose
conversation than to lyrical sonnets. The rhythms of *Middlemarch* are the rhythms of prose, long and irregular; and
the appetite of the book for a contemporary technical
vocabulary is an appetite that prose is well equipped to
satisfy. An electric battery, a disease of the retina, a jellyfish
– wanting to be able to include such prosy bits of the world,
Middlemarch, for the most part, resists any temptation to
lyric flight. It is not that the book does without rhetorical
figures; it is that the figures walk rather than soar. Here is the
last paragraph of the novel, a parting glance at Dorothea:

Her finely-touched spirit had still its fine issues, though they were
not widely visible. Her full nature, like that river of which Cyrus
broke the strength, spent itself in channels which had no great name
on the earth. But the effect of her being on those around her was incalculably diffusive: for the growing good of the world is partly
dependent on unhistoric acts; and that things are not so ill with you
and me as they might have been, is half owing to the number who lived
faithfully a hidden life, and rest in unvisited tombs.   ("Finale")

The force of this paragraph depends on subtle modulations of
metaphor, especially the metaphors of broken fluidity and
unseen glory. But the last sentence is representative of the
novel as a whole, in the way that it mutes the metaphor and
dissolves the lyric possibility into the careful prose: precise,
undemonstrative, slow. All those fastidious qualifications –
"not widely visible," "partly dependent," "not so ill," "half
owing," – keep the flow of language adjusted to the pace of
the novel's governing sensibility, the sensibility of the prose
pedestrian, slowing down to make sure that all the relevant
minutiae have been duly catalogued.

The beckoning of the ideal

And yet the question of realism remains unsettled, because in
Middlemarch the programmatic commitment to the ordinary,
the commonplace, and the familiar, is overlaid by a rival interest which has developed strongly in George Eliot's imagination. The essay "Silly Novels by Lady Novelists" (1856)

deals harshly with the self-indulgent fantasies of popular fiction, in which the perfectly ideal heroine

as often as not marries the wrong person to begin with, and she suffers terribly . . . but even death has a soft place in his heart for such a paragon, and remedies all mistakes for her just at the right moment. . . [The] tedious husband dies in his bed requesting his wife, as a particular favour to him, to marry the man she loves best, and having already dispatched a note to the lover informing him of the comfortable arrangement.

What is so striking about this disdainful description is how closely it predicts the narrative of Dorothea Brooke, George Eliot's own cherished paragon who also makes a bad marriage, suffers agonies, and is relieved by the opportune arrival of death. Of course in *Middlemarch* Casaubon does not complete the fantasied reversal. Instead of arranging for the second, happy marriage to Ladislaw, he attempts to prevent it through the cruel terms of his will. Here is the realist's refusal of idle fantasy, an insistence on the ugly facts that streak even the most beautiful life. But George Eliot's final turn against the formula of the "silly novelists" should not obscure the extent to which she relies on it. Many readers have felt that it is simply too convenient, too romantically providential, to have Casaubon die just instants before Dorothea binds her whole life to his fruitless labor. Such a fact — as also for instance the chance return of Raffles — does not transform *Middlemarch* into a silly novel but it does keep us from seeing it simply as the triumph of realism.

Specifically, it reminds us that even in a work as conspicuously realist as *Middlemarch* elements of wish-fulfillment creep softly in. It would be careless indeed to see the strong mark of fantasy as evidence that George Eliot fails in the pursuit of realism; far better to see it as a sign that her pursuit has more objects than one, that it is not strictly concerned — as her critical utterances easily suggest — with the "faithful representing of commonplace things" but that it seeks also to represent the uncommon, the abnormal, the epic, the magnificent. As the "Prologue" makes clear, the story of Dorothea Brooke will be a tale of "spiritual grandeur" caught and tangled in mediocrity, a tale of an epic character forced to walk in the middle march. It is clear that this interest in the ideal life strains against the commitment to a realism of the commonplace, and perhaps the best way to see the novel's reliance on the methods of popular fantasy – especially its reliance on the coincidence that allows Casaubon to die just in time to free Dorothea from years of useless toil – is as an effort to free its characters to aspire to the ideal. To have left Dorothea within the bonds of a strangulating marriage tie might have satisfied some stern notion of a fiercely unsentimental realism, but George Eliot, though she is stern, is also hopeful, and by murdering Casaubon so opportunely, she gives spiritual grandeur the chance to show its glory.

That the goodness of Dorothea exists in some tension with the usual canons of realism is a point made unambiguously clear, when the narrator remarks that "She was blind, you see, to many things obvious to others – likely to tread in the wrong places, as Celia had warned her; yet her blindness to whatever did not lie in her own pure purpose carried her safely by the side of precipices where vision would have been perilous with fear" (IV, 37).

As Graver (1984) has argued, George Eliot endures a tension between the desire to record facts and the longing to invoke ideals; in Graver's terms this leads to a strain between "idealism of conception and realism of presentation." When Dorothea tells Will Ladislaw about the "belief" that has regulated her life, the novel reaches towards its moral ideal:

That by desiring what is perfectly good, even when we don't quite know what it is and cannot do what we would, we are part of the divine power against evil – widening the skirts of light and making the struggle with darkness narrower.   (IV, 39)

The notion of the "perfectly good" is what animates so much of the novel, but the commitment to aesthetic realism, to the hard unalterable facts of the case, means that goodness is made to collide with unlovely circumstance. In comparing Lydgate to his illustrious scientific predecessors, the novel points out that each of his heroes "had his little local personal history sprinkled with small temptations and sordid cares, which made the retarding friction of his course towards final companionship with the immortals." With Lydgate, as with Dorothea, it is right to follow Graver and to see the epic life in opposition to a realist method that appropriates grandeur into the context of the local, the small, the sordid.

But a further ambiguity needs to be registered here, because it is not simply that ideal value contests realist fact; it is that fact has its own high value for George Eliot. Realism is not just an aesthetic method for her; it is an act of lofty moral engagement. In introducing Mary Garth, the narrator indicates that "honesty, truth-telling fairness, was Mary's reigning virtue: she neither tried to create illusions, nor indulged in them for her own behoof" (I, 12). And of Mrs. Garth, Mary's mother, we learn that "she had that rare sense which discerns what is inalterable, and submits to it without murmuring" (III, 24). The two Garth women represent strong instances of the moral realism which is one pole of the novel's ethical sense and which stands at a great distance from the opposing pole of moral idealism associated with Dorothea Brooke. The desire to acknowledge what we know to be true, to admit what is inevitable, to rid oneself of the temptation of illusions, and then, contrarily, the desire to ascend to perfect goodness, to pass beyond the bounds of what we know or can say, to refuse to submit to the apparently unalterable − the way of Mary Garth and the way of Dorothea Brooke, the honest ordinary sinner and the inspired secular saint − represent two distinct moral aspirations in the novel that place great strain on any fictional method attempting to contain them.

Plots and multi-plots

In the twenty-ninth chapter of the novel Dorothea and Casaubon, having recently returned from their honeymoon in Rome, quarrel over the prospect of a visit from Will Ladislaw and the awkward encounter leads directly to Casaubon's first physical attack. The next chapter sees the arrival of Lydgate who has an interview with Dorothea in order to discuss her husband's condition. The thirty-first chapter begins with Lydgate describing Dorothea to Rosamond; the chapter ends with their engagement and with Mr. Vincy's ready approval of the match, an approval explained in terms of Vincy's confidence that his son Fred will soon inherit Featherstone's fortune. The next two chapters follow the last days of Featherstone, the clutching cupidity of his relatives, the perversity of the old man himself, and the anguish of Mary Garth who refuses to tamper with his will even as he shrieks at her in the moments before his death. Chapter thirty-four is given to the funeral of Featherstone which is held in Lowick churchyard and is described from the perspective of Dorothea's family circle as they watch from the upper window of her home. As the chapter ends, Will Ladislaw makes an unexpected entrance; Dorothea turns pale; and Casaubon bows politely.

This sequence of six chapters offers a perfect illustration of the plotting of the novel. While George Eliot was willing to avail herself of the privileges that, for instance, Dickens so casually enjoyed – the privilege of leaping from one corner of the fictional canvas to another, of dropping one thread of narrative and abruptly picking up another – her preferred method was to obey a more fastidious scruple. The collapse of Casaubon leads to the arrival of Lydgate; Lydgate then becomes the focus of the narrative eye, carrying the plot up to his engagement; Mr. Vincy's assent is tied to the imminent demise of Featherstone; Featherstone's funeral at Lowick churchyard brings the story back to the Casaubon milieu. This movement, in which each episode naturally generates the next, is the counterpart in plot of the law-like regularity that George Eliot sees in the natural world.

"In watching effects," begins the fortieth chapter, "if only of an electric battery, it is often necessary to change our place and examine a particular mixture or group at some distance from the point where the movement we are interested in was set up" (IV, 40). The language of the laboratory is apt. Plot in *Middlemarch* unfolds much like the experiment of a chemist; episodes are regularly linked as effects to causes; and the activity of the narrator, as the quotation suggests, is to keep moving, to keep following the sequence of causes and the succession of effects. One is moved to ask: What gives coherence to the play of causes and effects? And what makes that question difficult is that the totality George Eliot seeks is not, as it is sometimes for Dickens, the vast expression of an underlying essence, the large manifestation of a simple truth; it is rather an infinitely complex, infinitely various, endlessly entangled web of human relations. The closer the approach to totality, the more tangled the web.

The basis for this aesthetic commitment − realism as totality, totality as complexity − lies in another of George Eliot's derivations from Victorian science. Sally Shuttleworth (1984) has recently called attention to an essay by Herbert Spencer called "Progress: Its Law and its Cause" (1857), which George Eliot would surely have known and which argues that the basis for all organic development is a movement from homogeneity to heterogeneity, unity to diversity, simplicity to complexity. As Shuttleworth goes on to point out, Spencer's view of development, a view that epitomizes a dominant Victorian scientific assumption, underlies the highly suggestive essay that George Eliot sketched in her notebook under the heading "Notes on Form in Art" (1868). The progress of artistic form, she argues there, is not toward simplicity; it is rather a relentless movement away from simplicity − toward internal differentiation, unlikeness, distinction, but always controlled by a sense of organic structure. The highest form, writes George Eliot, is

the relation of multiplex interdependent parts to a whole which is itself in the most varied & therefore the fullest relation to other wholes. Thus, the human organism comprises things as diverse as the finger-nails & tooth-ache, as the nervous stimulus of muscle manifested in a shout, & the discernment of a red spot on a field of snow; but all its different elements or parts of experience are bound together in a more necessary wholeness or more inseparable group of common conditions than can be found in any other existence known to us. The highest Form, then, is the highest organism, that is to say, the most varied group of relations bound together in a wholeness which again has the most varied relations with all other phenomena.

This is a highly abstract piece of argument well deserving a second and a third reading, but its importance to *Middlemarch* is highly concrete. The plotting of the novel is where the "multiplexity," the heterogeneity, may be seen most clearly. From the moment that the story called "Miss Brooke" became grafted on to the first version of *Middlemarch*, George Eliot showed her willingness to bring together sharply distinct plot lines, each requiring their own tones of voice, each provoking their own lines of moral reflection. The story of Fred Vincy, Camden Farebrother and the Garths; the story of Lydgate and Rosamond; the story of Bulstrode; the story of Dorothea, Casaubon and Will Ladislaw: these have their separate logic, their separate impulsions, driving them to their very distinct outcomes.

A mark of George Eliot's virtuosity, it is true, was her ability to wrap these separate strands together and to forestall the perception that she was forcing four different narratives into one long novel. When Lydgate finds his medical career fatally linked to the deceptions of Bulstrode, or when Will Ladislaw inadvertently becomes a lure for Rosamond, or when Dorothea sets herself to clear Lydgate's damaged reputation, the lines of plot intersect neatly. Readers of the novel have traditionally longed for still more convergence; Henry James regretted that "the current of [Lydgate's life] should not mingle more freely" with the stream of Dorothea's. But it was part of George Eliot's most well-meditated intention that the different parts of her narrative should respect the law of heterogeneity and that they should wind their way toward different ends. Gillian Beer (1983) connects this intention with Darwin's influence, which would have taught George Eliot a respect for diversity and variation; some individuals succeed, some fail; this is the inevitable result of the mixed conditions that accompany moral evolution as surely as they accompany the evolution of species.

Fred Vincy ends a happily married man; Lydgate dies in unappeased bitterness; Dorothea endures the chastening of her ambitions – these represent not only incongruent conclusions; they also represent divergent modes of storytelling. Fred Vincy's weakness, his disappointment, his chastening, his reformation, belong to the mode of gentle pastoral that George Eliot relied on, for instance, in *Silas Marner*. Set against this, the inexorable fall of both Lydgate and

Bulstrode is cast in the harsh, unsentimental tones of domestic tragedy, while the uncertain outcome of Dorothea's struggles exists within a hybrid literary genre, a kind of epic romance submitted to the corrosions of modern scepticism. The novel ends with its careful, nuanced appraisal of Dorothea's success-in-failure, but the solemn notes that end the novel cannot mute the other tones — the tone of happy pastoral and the tone of domestic tragedy — that have sounded just a few paragraphs earlier. Plots that once intersected have now disentangled themselves thoroughly; Graver is surely correct in saying that the complexity of George Eliot's fictional structure finally overwhelms her commitment to organic wholeness. The problem of incommensurable moral values — the value of Dorothea set next to the value of Mary Garth — is only made more acute by the problem of incommensurable plots. Can anything hold *Middlemarch* together?

This is the question that Henry James put to himself when he reviewed the novel on its first appearance. His answer is that the novel's diversity is held together by nothing more, nor less, than the width of its glance. *Middlemarch* is a "panorama." The choice of this particular term is notable, since nearly fifty years later when James's literary principles were codified by his disciple Percy Lubbock, "panorama" became a central descriptive term. In his *Craft of Fiction* Lubbock made an influential distinction between "scenic" and "panoramic" methods of narrative, which he put in these terms.

Are we placed before a particular scene, an occasion, at a certain selected hour in the lives of those people whose fortunes are to be followed? Or are we surveying their lives from a height, participating in the privilege of the novelist — sweeping their history with a wide range of vision and absorbing a general effect?

If the first, we are witnessing a scene; if the second, a panorama. As an example of the latter, Lubbock offers the case of Thackeray; this is reasonable but it is clear that the tendency toward panorama, toward sweeping general effects, works its way through much nineteenth-century fiction. One finds it in Dickens, in Trollope, and certainly, as James did, in George Eliot. The "Prelude" and the "Finale" to *Middlemarch* are epitomes of the panoramic impulse to be expansive, inclusive, totalizing.

It would be a mistake, though, to classify the narrative habits of this complex novel too definitively. The fifteenth chapter begins with a famous reflection on the sweeping view of Henry Fielding which is described as the charming manner of a bygone age. It was all very well for Fielding, but

> We belated historians must not linger after his example; and if we did so, it is probable that our chat would be thin and eager, as if delivered from a camp-stool in a parrot-house. I at least have so much to do unravelling certain human lots, and seeing how they were woven and interwoven that all the light I can command must be concentrated on this particular web, and not dispersed over the tempting range of relevancies called the universe.   (II, 15)

This commitment to the "particular web" must be seen as a counter-tendency to panorama. If it is clear that *Middlemarch* situates its events within the grand context of the "history of man," it is also clear that it rigorously concentrates on its highly particular contingencies. Moreover, as the novel unfolds and its historical, moral and emotional contexts are established, it gives increasingly focused attention to the immediate dramatics of its central figures: Bulstrode and Raffles, Will and Dorothea, Lydgate and Rosamond. The book closes with a series of great set-pieces that George Eliot had anticipated in her notebook: Dorothea "Finds Will with Rosamond"; "Will's outburst of bitterness against R."; "Dorothea's anguish & struggles"; "Wills [*sic*] interview with Dorothea: Reconciliation."

James's prestige aside, no one would call these moments "panoramic"; they are incontestably "scenic" in their concentrated focus; and indeed they prepare for some of James's own scenic triumphs. But to say this is only to make the larger formal difficulty more acute. If the panoramic view inexorably dissolves into these diverse strong scenes, we need to ask again: Can anything hold *Middlemarch* together?

The narrator

Another locus of value, another site of moral action, another resonant presence, must concern us now. This is the site occupied by the narrator of *Middlemarch*, the unnamed indeterminate garrulous voice that never enters the realm of action but becomes decisive to the experience of the book. Any reader's memory of *Middlemarch* must be in significant measure a memory of the narrator, who not only describes, narrates, and comments, but who also becomes as central a protagonist as any figure in the book.

The history of the European novel is, among other things, a history of its narrators, a history of narrative powers and privileges, and then also a history of narrative weaknesses and limitations. "Who that cares much to know the history of man" ("Prelude") − this is the phrase that opens *Middlemarch* and immediately suggests the ambitions of a narrator confident that nothing in human history will elude its searching view. The panoramic eye of the narrator is what the novel's characters tellingly lack; even the most visionary among them have blind spots in their field of view; the "short-sighted" Dorothea imagines people better than they are, while Lydgate is fatally incapable of studying ordinary life with the same rigor he brings to anatomy and physiology. And it is not simply that the narrator sees more, knows more, and understands more than the characters; it is that the seeing, knowing and understanding take place on another plane of experience entirely. "Poor Lydgate!" writes the narrator, "or shall I say, Poor Rosamond! Each lived in a world of which the other knew nothing" (II, 16). Here, as so often in *Middlemarch*, the narrator goes where no human being can ever tread: namely, into the intimate consciousness of other people. The crucial insight that Lydgate and Rosamond live in worlds unknown to each other is available only to someone who can stand outside the limits of human subjectivity, who can transcend finite individual experience and then from that transcendent perspective look down on the many subjective worlds that lie below. The ignorance of Lydgate and Rosamond is set against the full comprehension of the pitying narrator.

The "Finale" of *Middlemarch* begins with the narrator in a position of commanding authority, preparing to announce the final fates of the novel's characters.

Every limit is a beginning as well as an ending. Who can quit young lives after being long in company with them, and not desire to know what befell them in their after-years? For the fragment of a life, however typical, is not the sample of an even web: promises may not be kept, and an ardent outset may be followed by declension; latent powers may find their long-awaited opportunity; a past error may urge a grand retrieval.

What is most notable about this voice is its perfectly abstract equanimity. It is now speaking on a plane of supreme generality – the generality of beginnings and endings, youth and age, promises and powers, error and retrieval – as much to imply that there is no particular detail that can resist its assimilating powers. Indeed, this voice will go on to record the disparate destinies of Fred and Mary, Lydgate and Rosamond, Celia and James Chettam, Dorothea and Will, without breaking the consistency of its tone. Within the encompassing, comprehending, inclusive view of the narrator, such divergent temperaments as those of Dorothea and Mary are made to appear, not as conflicting principles of moral good, but merely as aspects of a totality that transcends them. This is also how Lydgate the embittered professional and Ladislaw the ardent politician appear – as well as the nobly self-denying Farebrother and the scarcely noble but always decent Fred Vincy. The narrator, in brief, aspires in such moments to become the agent of moral unity. Existing beyond the limits that obstruct the union of the characters, the narrator is the one who seems to exemplify most fully the great virtue associated with Dorothea: "the reaching forward of the whole consciousness towards the fullest truth, the least partial good" (II, 20).

"We are all of us born in moral stupidity, taking the world as an udder to feed our supreme selves" (II, 21) – "We judge from our own desires" (V, 53) – "we all of us, grave or light, get our thoughts entangled in metaphors, and act fatally on the strength of them" (I, 10) – each of these "we" sentences, like their many companions throughout the work, spreads the arms of generality in order to bring isolated individuals within a common perspective. The deceit, hypocrisy, and finally murderousness of Bulstrode risk turning him into a moral

monster, a grotesque exception to the common world. But the
narrator works with special intensity to bring even Bulstrode
within collective categories of moral understanding. Bulstrode

was simply a man whose desires had been stronger than his theoretic
beliefs, and who had gradually explained the gratification of his
desires into satisfactory agreement with those beliefs.   (VI, 61)

Bulstrode, in short, is one of us.

An abiding danger to the ethical universe of *Middlemarch*
is the falling away of human concern from the public world
into the abyss of the lonely ego. Left alone, we are unstable,
wavering creatures. And so the narrator scoffs at Bulstrode's
recourse to private religious devotion: "Does any one suppose that private prayer is necessarily candid – necessarily
goes to the roots of action. . . [Who] can represent himself
just as he is, even in his own reflections?" (VII, 70). It is the
task of the narrator to *represent* character as it cannot represent
itself – to stand outside the dangerous enclosure of self-
representations in order to secure the claims of the public
world. The twenty-ninth chapter of the novel begins with the
apparently unexceptional bit of narrative: "One morning,
some weeks after her arrival at Lowick, Dorothea. . ." – and
then suddenly the narrator makes a famous halt: "but why
always Dorothea? Was her point of view the only possible one
with regard to this marriage?" The answer of course is No, and
the chapter deserts the perspective of Dorothea in order to
plumb the recesses of Casaubon who "had an intense consciousness within him, and was spiritually a-hungered like the
rest of us. . . . For my part I am very sorry for him" (III, 29).
What Dorothea must acknowledge in order to emerge from
"moral stupidity," and this is perhaps the supreme act of
recognition in George Eliot's universe, is that another human
being (in her case Casaubon) has "an equivalent centre of self"
(II, 21), an equivalent intensity of consciousness. It is the
narrator who exemplifies this fundamental moral act by
continually escaping the confines of each particular subjectivity, by adopting new points of view, and by demonstrating
the rich plurality of consciousnesses that constitute our
world.

E. M. Forster wrote in *Aspects of the Novel* that what distinguishes a novel from life is that in a novel "we can know people perfectly," that their "secret lives are visible." *Middlemarch* can be taken as the epitome of this general resource in prose fiction, this capacity to open up the shell that surrounds consciousness and to bring it into a shared realm. To expose private consciousness and to multiply consciousnesses, these are the strong gestures toward the social world – toward the realm of interpersonal connection which the novel insistently puts before its would-be solitaries. As Elizabeth Deeds Ermarth (1985) has pointed out, the novel is populated not only by its many characters, but also by crowds of unnamed spectators – for instance the unspecified "others" in the town who dislike Bulstrode's aura of superiority. The novel is thus "populate[d] with invisible extras," and the result, as Ermarth puts it, is that "we are saved from solipsism by the inevitably social nature of consciousness." The narrator, having broken the spell of Dorothea's point of view, is free to evoke an infinite number of points of view and, in so doing, to situate the self firmly within its large society.

Yet, while George Eliot feels an absolute commitment to the social life, and to the necessity of social duties, she remains highly sceptical of the very society she asks her characters to serve. The collective mind that she so diligently constructs in her fiction is often an object of her bitter contempt. In her essay on "The Influence of Rationalism" (1865) she conjures an unflattering image of the "general reader" as one who

> may be known in conversation by the cordiality with which he assents to indistinct, blurred statements: say that black is black, he will shake his head and hardly think it; say that black is not so very black, he will reply, "Exactly" . . . His only bigotry is a bigotry against any clearly-defined opinion; not in the least based on a scientific scepticism, but belonging to a lack of coherent thought – a spongy texture of mind, that gravitates strongly to nothing. The one thing he is staunch for is, the utmost liberty of private haziness.

In *Middlemarch* the narrator strives sedulously to move from egoism toward the public world, but public opinion itself proves to be a coarse and vulgar instrument. The "common eyes" ("Prelude") that fail to recognize Dorothea's epic stature, the "general black-balling" (VIII, 74) that drives Lydgate out of Middlemarch, the requirement that "people [do] what their neighbors did" (I, 1) — these are all signs of an oppressive public mind that threatens to obliterate moral distinction. Dorothea's view that "the greater part of the world is mistaken about many things" (VI, 54) is also the view of the narrator. It is therefore much too simple to see the narrator's aim as leading the movement from private to public life, because public life poses its own deep dangers.

After recording the various low opinions held of Mr. Casaubon, the narrator cautions against "hasty judgment" and doubts whether even "the greatest man of his age, if ever that solitary superlative existed, could escape these unfavourable reflections of himself in various small mirrors":

Suppose we turn from outside estimates of a man, to wonder, with keener interest, what is the report of his own consciousness about his doings or capacity: with what hindrances he is carrying on his daily labours; what fading of hopes, or what deeper fixity of self-delusion the years are marking off within him; and with what spirit he wrestles against universal pressure, which will one day be too heavy for him, and bring his heart to its final pause.   (I, 10)

Casaubon, in sum, is "the centre of his own world" (I, 10), and it is this root truth which is quickly forgotten by a public opinion so pleased with its "outside estimates" and its "peremptory judgments." But to say this is to identify a second and contrary responsibility for the narrator, not a movement from egotism to the social sense, from private to public life, but now a movement from public back to private, from the distortions of the collective mind to the immediacy of lived subjective experience.

The complacency of "private prayer" and the complacency of public opinion — these are opposing threats in the novel which the narrator struggles to meet; the difficulty is that to respond to one is to risk surrendering to the other. The insistence on transcending the narrow view of the particular self in order to acknowledge a world of others risks overvaluing the public mind, the general reader. But to turn away from public opinion is to risk the illusions of self-infatuation. There is no easy or stable solution to this dilemma. The narrator tries alternately to rouse the social sense and to preserve the self against the encroachments of public opinion.

This division of narrative labor underlies the division of narrative voice well described by Ermarth, who plausibly claims that the reader can hear two distinct voices, one of "generalized historical awareness" and one that is "intermittently personalized." In rough terms the difference may be associated with the voice which says "I" – "I am very sorry for [Casaubon]" – and the voice which says "We": "We are all of us born in moral stupidity." The former works to defend personality from the moral absorptions of public conformity; the latter works to protect the community from the temptations of egoism. And because these functions are so clearly distinct, because the narrator turns so sharply from the cause of community to the cause of subjectivity, no unity can be sustained. The synthesis of tone and the synthesis of moral aspiration cannot contain the pressures toward variation – variation in moral value, in literary mode, in plot, and in voice.

Unity or sympathy?

The word poised at the center of George Eliot's aesthetic as of her moral doctrine is "sympathy," a word that retains for her a rich power of implication far beyond our pale ordinary uses of the term. In *Middlemarch* as in her critical writings, it suggests a fundamental human gesture – an overwhelming of instinctive egoism, a turning outward to the world beyond the self, a meeting and a mingling and a merging with another self, another center of another world.

In 1866, Frederic Harrison, a friend of George Eliot and one of the leading English exponents of Comte's positivism, proposed that she write a novel illustrating the perfect society that Comte's theories could bring into being. George Eliot admitted the attraction of the project, but she worried that it would turn a novel into a "diagram" and that it would appeal to the scientific mind but would not lead the emotions to an "aroused sympathy." As she put it bluntly in a letter of 1859, "If Art does not enlarge men's sympathies, it does nothing morally," and three years earlier, in her essay on "The Natural History of German Life," she wrote that "The greatest benefit we owe to the artist, whether painter, poet, or novelist, is the extension of our sympathies."

Community for George Eliot depends most importantly not on principle, doctrine, or law, but on the binding ties of sympathy — where sympathy is understood not as thoughtless emotionalism, but as a union of thought and emotion — feeling regulated by ideas, ideas animated by feeling. Moreover, the notion that communal solidarity depends on sympathetic acts becomes a basis for the realist aesthetic. The narrator of *Adam Bede* holds that

It is more needful that I should have a fibre of sympathy connecting me with that vulgar citizen who weighs out my sugar . . . more needful that my heart should swell with loving admiration at some trait of gentle goodness in the faulty people who sit at the same hearth with me . . . than at the deeds of heroes whom I shall never know.(II, 17)

A realist literature, in this view, is in the service of social solidarity just to the extent that in recording the characters and events of common life it teaches affection for the ordinary.

But part of the stress on George Eliot's realism is that, though she never abandoned the ideal of sympathy for the ordinary sinner, she came increasingly to realize how *extraordinary* was the genuinely sympathetic soul. Service to common life remained the inspiring ambition, but by the time of *Middlemarch* the question was whether fidelity to commonplace things was possible for any but those, in Dorothea's words, who achieved "a higher life than the common" (VIII, 76). It is Dorothea herself, and Dorothea virtually alone, who consistently achieves this uncommon sympathy for common existence, whose life is swept along in a "full current of sympathetic motive" (I, 10). When Lydgate reaches his great crisis, he discovers in Dorothea's confidence "the exquisite sense of leaning entirely on a generous sympathy, without any check of proud reserve" (VIII, 76). Certainly the moral climax of the book occurs when Dorothea believes that Will has betrayed her with Rosamond, and she falls into "burning scorn," into "jealous indignation and disgust." Through the intense meditation of a long night, she forces herself "to dwell on every detail" and ask herself, "Was she alone in that scene? Was it her event only? She forced herself to think of it as bound up with another woman's life. . ." At the end of this momentous inner struggle, "all [her] vivid sympathetic experience returned to her now as a power" (VIII, 80), and in resolving "to see and save Rosamond," in extending the current of feeling until it reaches the characters least capable of feeling sympathy, Dorothea becomes George Eliot's most perfect exemplar of the moral life.

It is not too much to say that what Dorothea achieves through her night of agony, George Eliot wants us to achieve through our nights of reading *Middlemarch*. Strenuous as the imaginative labor may be, the task of the reader is to grow beyond moral stupidity and to discover an active sympathetic relationship to even the most unattractive characters. Raffles, Featherstone, and Bulstrode are often intensely repellent, and repellent by design, but the reading of the book is meant to be a training of the emotions that will bring them into our universe of feeling. The capacity to develop a roving sympathy that can turn like a beacon and that can illuminate whatever it sees — this is what the book exhibits and what it teaches: a roving sympathy that is not to be confused with unity. Indeed it is the test of sympathy in George Eliot that it can accept disunity, that it can discover various responses to the various demands of human weakness. For all the talk in her criticism of the organic wholeness of a work of literature, *Middlemarch* is not held together finally by some overarching moral perspective; it is held together by *our* learning to perform many and diverse acts of sympathy. This is the moral of its method: that art, like human community, should seek not a unity that can reconcile life's multiplex variety, but should seek instead a sympathy prepared to adjust to all the irregularities of the human landscape.

Chapter 3

Middlemarch and the art of living well

Many selves, one life

The moral act described at the end of the previous chapter — the crossing of a threshold from egoism into altruism, the acknowledgment of other centers of living subjectivity, the release of sympathetic emotion — is no doubt the fundamental gesture of *Middlemarch*, as it is the fundamental gesture in George Eliot's ethical vision. But that fundamental gesture is not easy for anyone to make. For George Eliot, it is not simply the product of a strong resolve, or a firm decision, or a decisive act of will. The moral life for her is enshrined because it is moral but no less because it is a life, because it develops in time — or, as the narrator tersely puts it, "character too is a process and an unfolding" (II, 15). This thought is refined in an important exchange between Dorothea and Farebrother on the question of Lydgate's alleged role in Bulstrode's murder of Raffles. When Dorothea begins to defend Lydgate by saying that "there is a man's character beforehand to speak for him," Farebrother responds tellingly that "character is not cut in marble — it is not something solid and unalterable. It is something living and changing, and may become diseased as our bodies do." Then, answers Dorothea, "it may be rescued and healed" (VIII, 72).

Bulstrode is the novel's strongest example of the slow disease that eats away moral character. The narrator repeatedly emphasizes the fact that one can point to no single moment when Bulstrode turned from a life of principle to an act of crime. Instead he allowed himself a series of minor compromises and subtle lapses that the narrator shrewdly compares to a gradual relaxing of the muscles. The result is that "the train of causes in which he had locked himself" (VI, 61) works inexorably toward the murder of Raffles. In the case of Lydgate there is nothing so spectacular at the end of the train of causes, but for him too there is a sequence of apparently trivial concessions until he finds himself "sliding into that pleasureless yielding to the small solicitations of circumstance, which is a commoner history of perdition than any single momentous bargain" (VIII, 79). This opposition between the "small solicitations" and the "momentous bargain" is essential in the novel, and it lies behind George Eliot's reinterpretation of the possibilities for moral action.

"Our lives," we read in *Romola*, "make a moral tradition for our individual selves, as the life of mankind at large makes a moral tradition for the race; and to have once acted nobly seems a reason why we should always be noble" (II, 39). Of the two aspects in this aphorism pertinent to *Middlemarch*, a first is the notion that to lead a life is to construct a moral tradition: to act is always to create precedents, habits, and dispositions that will guide future action. And if to act nobly is to increase the chance of future nobility, *Middlemarch* shows clearly that to act meanly is to nourish a tradition of meanness. When Bulstrode blinds himself to the incompatibility between his religious belief and his handling of stolen goods, he prepares himself for later, more catastrophic, blindnesses. A decision in the present is determined by a history of decisions, and no act of will can ever be strong enough to obliterate the constraints of its past.

What gives dramatic force to this idea of a continuous moral tradition, however, is the extent to which modern lives seem *discontinuous*. In a book called *George Eliot and Blackmail*, Alexander Welsh has shown how central to her fiction is the motif of the discontinuous life, how often characters experience a violent rupture dividing their lives into radically separate parts. Again, Bulstrode is only the most conspicuous example; Dorothea, Will, and Lydgate all endure various forms of disconnection and discontinuity. And in accounting for this recurrent pattern, Welsh connects it with the social mobility of the Victorian middle class that permitted, indeed encouraged, the discontinuity that arises from changing one's social position — and in particular, from changing one's vocation. Bulstrode's move from morally tainted pawnbroker to respectable banker, Lydgate's move from the privileges of high birth to the responsibilities of a provincial doctor, Ladislaw's move from aspiring painter to aspiring politician, Fred Vincy's hesitation between the church and the farm, Farebrother's feeling that he was not meant to be a vicar − all these instances suggest the difficulty of finding a secure vocational commitment; and they equally suggest the instability of a social order that offers individuals no fixed place within it.

And yet for George Eliot, one might say, discontinuity is no excuse. Change can only mask, it cannot erase, the underlying tradition of an individual life. Characters may seek to cross the definitive threshold and to put their past securely behind them. This is just the temptation encouraged by an unstable society. But *Middlemarch* reveals that temptation as only another dangerous fantasy: discontinuity is what its characters often desire, but continuity is what they inevitably find. When Will and Dorothea believe that their connection has to end and that they are parting irrevocably, the narrator sagely reminds the reader that they are young and that

> no age is so apt as youth to think its emotions, partings, and resolves are the last of their kind. Each crisis seems final, simply because it is new. We are told that the oldest inhabitants in Peru do not cease to be agitated by the earthquakes, but they probably see beyond each shock, and reflect that there are plenty more to come.   (VI, 55)

Indeed, Will and Dorothea have crises ahead: it is Will's particular habit to stride firmly away only to come sauntering back. The general point, enforced throughout the novel, is that tradition persists through crisis; there are many thresholds in the long corridor of a life: "Every limit is a beginning as well as an ending" ("Finale").

Bulstrode *means* to achieve a discontinuous life, *means* to make a violent break with his past and to achieve a new life. But with the return of John Raffles: "Into this second life Bulstrode's past had now risen" (VI, 61). Raffles is the living embodiment of a past that refuses to drop out of the moral tradition of Bulstrode's life.

> The terror of being judged sharpens the memory: it sends an inevitable glare over that long-unvisited past which has been habitually recalled only in general phrases. Even without memory, the life is

bound into one by a zone of dependence in growth and decay; but intense memory forces a man to own his blameworthy past. With memory set smarting like a reopened wound, a man's past is not simply a dead history, an outworn preparation of the present. . . it is a still quivering part of himself, bringing shudders and bitter flavours and the tinglings of a merited shame.   (VI, 61)

Much as Bulstrode learns that there is no "second life" but a life "bound into one," so Casaubon realizes that his engagement to Dorothea has failed to stir him emotionally, and so Lydgate, who had assumed that he had left his rebellious sexuality behind him in France, finds it again (more decorous, but also more conclusive) in Rosamond's drawing room. In a bitterly comic example, Bulstrode learns of Raffles that the "difference between his morning and evening [drunken] self was not so great as [Bulstrode] had imagined that it might be" (V, 53).

The discontinuous self, suggests *Middlemarch*, is only a myth of personality encouraged by a modern society that mythically believes in sudden transformation. On the political plane the Reform Bill is the great example of social discontinuity, but it is one of the novel's purposes to insist on the slow rhythms of history that underlie the surface perturbations. The Reform Bill, suggests the novel, is no more final than an earthquake in Peru. In an evocative phrase the narrator speaks of "the suppressed transitions which unite all contrasts" (II, 20), and the thought applies equally to personal and political life. This is the particular burden of contemporary existence; with all the change that it makes possible − change of place, change of spouse, change of work, change of moral or religious belief − it cannot free us from the need to "own" the past.

Public opinion, public crime

The discontinuity of experience set atop the moral tradition of the self creates a severe instability in the world of *Middlemarch*. Characters aspire to a new future only to discover that they are held responsible for the past; and here a second strain in Welsh's argument becomes pertinent, the claim that the problem of *reputation* takes on extraordinary new resonance in the work of George Eliot. In the extreme case of Bulstrode, this turns into the problem of blackmail, but as Welsh aptly notes, such characters as Casaubon, Dorothea, Will, Lydgate — and in a comic vein, Fred Vincy — are all faced with the threat of a fatally damaged reputation. The reception of Casaubon's life work, Dorothea's attachment to Will, Lydgate's involvement with Raffles' death, and the revelation of Ladislaw's parentage — in each instance, the danger is cast not in terms of physical or legal threat but in terms of the threat posed by that amorphous new entity, Public Opinion.

With detectable bitterness the narrator comments early in the novel that "Sane people did what their neighbours did, so that if any lunatics were at large, one might know and avoid them" (I, 1). D. A. Miller has pointed to the acts of stern suppression by a community that sees individual difference as a dangerous provocation. Public opinion, especially in the form of gossip, is the weapon wielded by the community against the strong protagonist. As Will says to Lydgate, "I shall be fortunate if gossip does not make me the most disreputable person in the whole affair. I should think the latest version must be, that I plotted with Raffles to murder Bulstrode, and ran away from Middlemarch for the purpose" (VIII, 79). And Lydgate notes how, as the rumors spread, he is treated "as if [he] were a leper" (VIII, 73). George Eliot takes great pains to emphasize that Bulstrode is entirely safe from the law; no crime could be formally tied to him; and yet the emphasis on his legal immunity is a way to dramatize the powers of a public opinion that awaits no official judgment before executing harsh decrees.

What is striking in all of this is that for all George Eliot's yearning toward an organic community in which every member contributes to the harmonious social body, in *Middlemarch* the portrait of community is a portrait of a failed community. It fails because it fails to know and, still more fundamentally, fails to sympathize. What the narrator calls "the general mind" is a mind that remains superstitious, uncritical, erratic, unsound, ungenerous. Having noted that there is no evidence of Lydgate's guilt in the death of Raffles, the narrator continues:

But this vague conviction of indeterminable guilt, which was enough to keep up much head-shaking and biting innuendo even among substantial professional seniors, had for the general mind all the superior power of mystery over fact. Everybody liked better to conjecture how the thing was, than simply to know it; for conjecture soon became more confident than knowledge, and had a more liberal allowance for the incompatible. Even the more definite scandal concerning Bulstrode's earlier life was, for some minds, melted into the mass of mystery, as so much lively metal to be poured out in dialogue, and to take such fantastic shapes as heaven pleased.   (VII, 71)

Middlemarch broods everywhere on the distinction between knowledge and opinion -- or as it is put here, knowledge and conjecture -- and the great danger with opinion is not that it is always wrong but that even when it is right -- as in the case of Bulstrode -- it is, as it were, accidentally right, right without principle, right without sympathy. This is why the general mind that can correctly condemn Bulstrode is also capable of the unfair and catastrophic condemnation of Lydgate.

When Dorothea rallies to Lydgate's defense, she says, "I feel convinced that his conduct has not been guilty: I believe that people are almost always better than their neighbours think they are." Then she adds, "People glorify all sorts of bravery except the bravery they might show on behalf of their nearest neighbours" (VIII, 72). This is a scathing indictment of community, and it is well worth puzzling over the fact that George Eliot, the apostle of the new humanist community, the great novelist of the communal life, can be so fiercely uncompromising in her repudiation of the common mind.

It is easy to read the "Finale" of *Middlemarch* as simply a charting of individual fates set against individual hopes. The narrator tells us what will become of Fred and Mary, Lydgate and Rosamond, Dorothea and Will. But the "Finale" is more than a meditation on these individual fates; it is also a last meditation on the general mind and its crippling misapprehensions. We learn in a mild and harmless example that Middlemarchers assume that Mary is responsible for the virtues in Fred's books on farming and also that "every one in the town" gave Fred credit for her tales of great men. More importantly, we find that the world considers Lydgate a success, while he regards his life as an unambiguous failure; and most seriously, we discover that Dorothea's excellences go unrecognized in the wider community.

A passage that appeared in the "Finale" of the first edition of the novel is gloomily explicit on this point.

Among the many remarks passed on [Dorothea's] mistakes, it was never said in the neighbourhood of Middlemarch that such mistakes could not have happened if the society into which she was born had not smiled on propositions of marriage from a sickly man to a girl less than half his own age — on modes of education which make a woman's knowledge another name for motley ignorance — on rules of conduct which are in flat contradiction with its own loudly-asserted beliefs. While this is the social air in which mortals begin to breathe, there will be collisions such as those in Dorothea's life, where great feelings will take the aspect of error, and great faith in the aspect of illusion.

The book, in short, paints an image of fallen community, fallen into a modernity that can neither recognize nor accommodate a "higher life than the common" (VIII, 76). Given such sentiments, and given such a sceptical reading of the integrity of community, it is easy to read *Middlemarch* as finally a resigned and even pessimistic book that measures the extent of our fall from the "coherent social faith" that had once made saintliness possible. But this would be too hasty a conclusion.

Time and social hope

In the earlier years of her writing career, the broad tone of George Eliot's social thought was a tone of hopeful resolution. A letter of 1853 gives a characteristic sentiment:

Is it not cheering to think of the youthfulness of this little planet, and the immensely greater youthfulness of our race upon it? — to think that the Higher moral tendencies of human nature are yet only in their germ?

It is true that by the time of *Middlemarch* George Eliot's historical cheerfulness was somewhat chastened, but it is also true that she never abandoned her sense of ongoing historical process, with the further implication that the condition of the present is only a moment in a vast temporal process.

To begin to see the bearing of this historical assumption on *Middlemarch*, it is worth considering the novel's treatment of the coming of the railways. When Solomon Featherstone realizes that he stands to make money by selling his land to the railway, he develops a plan to stimulate public opposition to the railways in order to raise the value of his property – at which point the narrator observes that "This reasoning of Mr. Solomon's was perhaps less thorough than he imagined, his cunning bearing about the same relation to the course of railways as the cunning of a diplomatist bears to the general chill or catarrh of the solar system" (VI, 56). What is striking about this choice of simile is the way George Eliot links the historical inevitability of the railway system to the physical laws that govern the solar system; the notion of interfering with the railways is as barren and futile as the notion of manipulating the movement of the planets. Soon after this, the book records a narrowly averted conflict between some railway workers and a group of misguided locals ready to attack them. Fred Vincy and Caleb Garth come to the aid of the workers, and after tempers settle, Caleb turns to the Middlemarchers and says, "Now, my lads, you can't hinder the railroad: it will be made whether you like it or not. . . Somebody told you the railroad was a bad thing. That was a lie. It may do a bit of harm here and there, to this and to that; and so does the sun in heaven. But the railway's a good thing" (VI, 56).

Two aspects of this episode should be noted. First is the studied *naturalizing* of history in the comparisons of the railroad to the solar system and then to the sun itself. The effect of this is to assimilate human history to the workings of nature, and to endow history with the inevitability of natural process. From the perspective of 1870, those who opposed the railway forty years earlier are rendered as deluded provincials who were incapable of grasping the necessary change. Additionally, the episode suggests that the narrowness of the Middlemarch community, though fatal to the hopes of Lydgate and Dorothea, is no permanent obstacle – it too must yield to the necessities of time.

The role of Caleb Garth is the second notable aspect of this sequence. Garth's high value within the moral scheme of the work is the value of a conservative. He conserves the values of an agrarian tradition, the values of land, labor, and quiet moral dignity. In no plausible respect is he a modern man. And yet, though Caleb Garth is the novel's great conservative, he is the one who accepts the coming of the railways – the one, that is, who embraces a form of modernization that might seem incompatible with his worship of the earth. But for George Eliot it is precisely Caleb's archaism that allows him to see beyond the blinded present. The fact that he belongs to the social past liberates him from the fallen present and binds him to the emerging future.

According to the demanding temporal logic of the novel, the past is in moral alliance with the future. The "Prelude" of the novel recalls the "coherent social faith" allowing St. Theresa to attain her epic life and then, in a difficult phrase, it adds that such faith "performed the function of knowledge for the ardently willing soul." The suggestion is that the crucial need is knowledge, and the implication must be that even after an age of faith, knowledge might find another form of coherence. Faith that has been, a coherent knowledge yet to be – we live between these termini. Recognition of this untethered condition is a large part of the novel's response to the fallen community: things have not always been so; and still more happily, they needn't always remain so. Knowledge in the future will give us (may give us) what faith gave in the past: a broad communal understanding of life that will nurture possibilities for individual moral grandeur. This is a refined notion of a collective moral tradition, not a smooth transmission of values but a halting erratic process beset by interruptions. The hostility to the railroad, the refusal of up-to-date medical treatments, the attempts to block medical reform – all are instances of temporary impediments that have to be swept away; and each example reminds us that history moves on remorselessly. By historicizing the events of the novel so thoroughly, George Eliot prevents a resigned acceptance of the status quo. It is not that *Middlemarch* implies some bland progress toward a reformed social life; it often reminds us of the failure of 1870 to grow beyond 1830; but the general insistence on historical change always keeps alive the possibility of the future triumph of a knowledge merged with sympathy.

Middlemarch makes yet another response to the failure of organic community, a response that does not depend on postponing satisfactions until some indeterminate future time. If social life as represented by the Middlemarch community never achieves an integrity that would bind its careening parts, there yet remains the small circles of family friends where it is possible to achieve true emotional solidarity. The Garth family has an easy pastoral stability, all teasing and tumbling and generous affection; and despite the lingering tensions between James Chettam and Will Ladislaw the families of Dorothea and Celia are "made whole again" ("Finale"). This is just what the larger society cannot achieve; it discovers temporary meretricious unities created through gossip, and then it falls back into the usual divisions.

Here we confront one of the difficulties in bringing *Middlemarch* within the usual categories of prose fiction. It is that while history makes such a large part of its subject, the novel bears scant resemblance to the defining examples of historical fiction, to the work of Scott, Tolstoy, and Stendhal. Indeed, surveys of the historical novel characteristically ignore *Middlemarch*, and it is not hard to see why. Both the literary practice and the critical understanding of the historical novel have tended to require an overt link between private lives and public events, so that when a novel records intimate personal details, these are taken to receive a deep significance from their connection to the political world. The destiny of nations, the unfolding of large-scale social movements, war and revolution -- such events need not be omnipresent, but they stand as warrant for the historical claims of the fiction. The claim on the reader made by Walter Scott's Edward Waverly is inseparable from his participation in the Jacobite Rebellion. George Eliot's own *Romola* is a classic instance of the insertion of private destiny within public fate. What imbues Romola herself with moral aura is precisely her involvement with real personages, such as Savonarola, Machiavelli, Piero di Cosimo, and with the real forces and tendencies that they represent.

Middlemarch reverses the priority established by Scott and his successors, and in this sense it stands as a critique of the norms of the historical novel. It is not that private lives receive their significance insofar as they are implicated in public events. On the contrary, public events are conceived as the product of small-scale private events; the spirit of history is something that stirs inside individuals; and while George Eliot does not deny that social circumstances have their own powerful reality, it is no more powerful than the individual circumstances that lie beyond the public eye. Will Ladislaw reflects that "the little waves make the large ones and are of the same pattern" (V, 46), and for the George Eliot of *Middlemarch* history is not essentially large, public, and external; it is something that runs through private life. George IV is no more deeply "historical" than Rosamond Vincy, and in focusing on her "particular web" of lives, George Eliot sees those lives as causes as much as effects.

It is this revaluation of historical fiction that helps to explain why the historical hope in the novel falls so frequently on the individual. Indeed in *Middlemarch* the supreme value of wholeness comes to settle, not on the community, but on the self. And where the community comes to seem small against the vast background of past and future, the individual (if her name is Dorothea) can seem as large as history itself. Toward the end of the novel Dorothea asks Lydgate to confide in her, to tell what he has had no audience to hear; and at this point we read:

Lydgate turned, remembering where he was, and saw Dorothea's face looking up at him with a sweet trustful gravity. The presence of a noble nature, generous in its wishes, ardent in its charity, changes the lights for us: we begin to see things again in their larger, quieter masses, and to believe that we too can be seen and judged in the wholeness of our character. (VIII, 76)

Soon after, when Dorothea speaks again, the narrator reports that, "The childlike grave-eyed earnestness with which Dorothea said all this was irresistible -- blent into an adorable whole with her ready understanding of high experience" (VIII, 76). These two passages, like so many others, help make clear that for George Eliot the prospect of "blending"individual responses into an "adorable whole" – adorable in its strong etymological sense, worthy of adoration -- begins to take the place of the wholeness once sought in communal life.

At this point a minor difficulty in the reading of *Middlemarch* should be mentioned. It can be best raised in regard to two minor characters, Dorothea's sister Celia and Humphrey Cadwallader, the Rector of Tipton and Freshitt. What the two characters share is, to put it most briefly, a good disposition unstreaked by malignity. No unkind thought ever passes through Celia's mind; she is ever "amiable"; and as for Cadwallader, who is the more complex case, he retains his tolerance, his cheerfulness, his "solid imperturbable ease and good-humour" (I, 8), even when all his intimates have lost theirs. In this respect the characters might seem to qualify as examples of that moral "whole" to which the entire novel tends. And yet, as readers of the novel come uneasily to realize, these two amiable figures are clearly marked as morally insufficient. In the great test case of Dorothea's engagement to Will Ladislaw, both Celia and Cadwallader, to their credit, refuse to join in the general condemnation. They remain benignly tolerant, but as *Middlemarch* sternly suggests, benignity is not enough. Of Cadwallader, the narrator comments that "His conscience was large and easy, like the rest of him: it did only what it could do without any trouble" (I, 8). And when Celia finally accepts the idea of Dorothea's marriage to Will and thinks "that it would be pleasant to hear the story," Dorothea refuses to tell. Instead she says, with gentle finality, "No, dear, you would have to feel with me, else you would never know" (VIII, 84). As these passages suggest, in the persons of Cadwallader and Celia, George Eliot seems intent to put goodness itself in question, to ask, in effect, whether being good is good enough.

A remark by Montaigne, in the essay "Of Cruelty" (1580), speaks directly to this issue. "It seems to me," he writes, "that virtue is something other and nobler than the indications toward goodness that are born in us." Virtue

means something greater and more active than letting oneself, by a happy disposition, be led gently and peacefully in the footsteps of reason. He who through a natural mildness and easygoingness should despise injuries received would do a very fine and praiseworthy thing; but he who, outraged and stung to the quick by an injury, should arm himself with the arms of reason against this furious appetite for vengeance, and after a great conflict should finally master it, would without doubt do much more. The former would do well, and the other virtuously; one action might be called goodness, the other virtue. For it seems that the name of virtue presupposes difficulty and contrast, and that it cannot be exercised without opposition.

Middlemarch offers the same understanding of Celia and Humphrey Cadwallader; it allows them goodness but deprives them of virtue. In the fiction of many of George Eliot's Victorian contemporaries, who preferred clearer separations between heroes and villains, it would be unreasonable to ask more of a character than that he or she be "good." But *Middlemarch* follows the insights of Montaigne in establishing a subtle continuum that disarms moral dualism; "good" and "bad" give way to various degrees and kinds of "better" and "worse." It also follows Montaigne, perhaps unconsciously, perhaps not, in its image of the workings of virtue, in its metaphors for the act of virtue. In one of the climactic moments in the moral life of Dorothea and therefore in the life of the novel, she is wounded by Casaubon's cold refusal of her sympathy; she falls toward the abyss of marital estrangement ("In such a crisis as this, some women begin to hate"); and then through an act of self-transformation which echoes the teaching of Montaigne, Dorothea begins the long movement from goodness to virtue:

. . . the struggle changed continually, as that of a man who begins with a movement towards striking and ends with conquering his desire to strike. The energy that would animate a crime is not more than is wanted to inspire a resolved submission, when the noble habit of the soul reasserts itself.   (IV, 42)

This is virtue, for George Eliot as for Montaigne: not the smooth expansion of a moral instinct, but the anguished challenge to the self by the self. It might even be said that in *Middlemarch* the self *becomes* the community that cannot be realized in social terms. Early in the book we learn that

Dorothea "did not want to deck herself with knowledge – to wear it loose from the nerves and blood that fed her action" (I, 10); and after Casaubon's death, she comes to dread a life in which "her own energy" is unable to find "reasons for ardent action" (VI, 54). It is characteristic of George Eliot's fictional psychology to render the personality as an arena of warring emotions, faculties, and propensities, to portray it as a battle of "blood," "nerves," "knowledge," "energy," "reasons," "ardour," and "action." In the course of the work these carefully distinguished aspects of individual experience come to function like so many citizens of a republic: they contend, negotiate, wage civil war, and finally cause the wreck of personality (as in Bulstrode) or its hard-won triumph (as in Dorothea). If *Middlemarch* remains sceptical about the possibility of reconciling the various forces of contemporary social life, it is at least hopeful about the chances for reconciliation in the metaphoric community constituted within the complex self.

In its most explicit judgments, the novel is in staunch opposition to what it calls, in reference to Ladislaw, "self-culture" (V, 46). Nevertheless, a large part of the imaginative labor of the book is precisely to cultivate the self, and to perfect an image of moral individuality, with all its faculties brought into energetic harmony, its emotions and reasons dancing together, its beliefs blending with its blood. When *Middlemarch* is finally, regretfully, closed, its lingering positive images are not of social achievements, or even of family harmonies, but rather images of harmonious individuals – Dorothea, Caleb and Mary Garth, Farebrother – and the would-be harmony of the dissonant Lydgate. A reason for this turn to the self is suggested in a description of Bulstrode's attempt to rationalize his immorality:

This implicit reasoning is essentially no more peculiar to evangelical belief than the use of wide phrases for narrow motives is peculiar to Englishmen. There is no general doctrine which is not capable of eating out our morality if unchecked by the deep-seated habit of direct fellow-feeling with individual fellow-men.   (VI, 61)

As the passage makes clear, "general doctrine" suggests more than religious doctrine; it suggests any moral position that abstracts from individual experience and insists on universal principles. Certainly a powerful tradition in modern ethics, a tradition epitomized by the ethics of Immanuel Kant, holds that the very basis of morality is the general law – general laws making no concessions to individual need. But within English thought there stands a lineage running counter to the dominant Kantian tradition; it is associated with the philosophy of David Hume; and it holds, following Hume, that the essence of morality is not universal law, not abstract principle, but instead the gradual and unsteady movement from self-love to love of another. Instead of seeing the basic moral act as the development of a general doctrine, for Hume the basic act is the extension of our emotions from the original seat in the self. For Kant the desires of the individual are essentially antagonistic to morality, but for Hume morality begins in desire. Morality is desire that is tutored, trained, and steadily broadened.

George Eliot certainly felt the attraction of the grand Kantian picture of universal moral law, but her own moral sense began in the Humean recognition that morality begins at home, in the ego and its immediate environs. As she wrote to Oscar Browning during the writing of *Middlemarch* in 1870,

One must care for small immediate results as well as for great and distant ones – and in my own mind nothing takes greater emphasis than the possibility of being certain that our own character and deeds make a few lives near to us better than they would have been without our presence in the world.

The wholeness of character toward which *Middlemarch* aims is no fetish of private satisfaction – at least it is not meant as such; it is a wholeness that prepares to brim over into the lives of others, as Dorothea exudes her goodness to immerse Rosamond in their climactic scene together. In the last sentences of the book, we reach the complicated fate of the whole self. Dorothea's "full nature" meets the varied obstacles of her place and time, and her fulness divides "in channels." But if this deprives her of epic stature, it also allows her influence to be "incalculably diffusive," spreading its benignities into a world much in need of them. What this carefully wrought final passage makes clear is that the wholeness of the self, so difficult to achieve, is no resting point; it is a preparation for emanations, even at the expense of the "adorable whole" that is the noble self. If *Middlemarch* keeps returning to the ego, even as it sternly demands "fellow-feeling," this is because for George Eliot, as for the tradition she inherits, the place where one contests egoism is within the ego itself. The fundamental drama takes place within the individual psyche, as it prepares itself to overcome the cultivation of its own desires and to study the desires of others. For George Eliot, this is where morality begins, in the moment when the self turns against itself, contests itself, upbraids itself, and from within the ego conquers its egoism, achieving "self-forgetful ardour." We might say that this big novel exists in order to display that little step, the first step of the moral life when we cross the inner threshold between self-delight and self-overcoming.

Chapter 4

Gender and generation

Beyond the goose and gander

No issue in the interpretation of *Middlemarch* has been more consistently vexing than the representation of gender. For early (especially male) readers, the book failed to offer a strong masculine protagonist; for recent (especially female) readers the novel fails to acknowledge the strength in its women. It has been common for readers to feel (and to say) that in the person of Dorothea the novel creates an image of the feminist protagonist, but then, out of fear, doubt, weariness, or pessimism, George Eliot is unable to carry through the strength of her insight. She marries Dorothea to Will Ladislaw, of whom it has been said, since the first publication of the novel, that he is no fit match; and then in a final indignity the revolutionary possibilities contained in the portrait of Dorothea are renounced in favor of the conventional roles of wife and mother.

The challenges contained in this view must be met, but this will only be possible once the context of the issue has been set out fully. In order to do this, it will help to hold the question of Will and Dorothea in suspense and to bring forward the no less vexing question of Rosamond Vincy. The puzzle is not about Rosamond herself. The portrait is if anything too clearly drawn. The puzzle concerns the pronounced animus, the sustained hostility, that governs the narrator's relation to the character. In the case of Dorothea, one of the chief aims of the novel's commentary is to offer extenuations of her failures, to place her weaknesses, her mistakes, and her limitations within a social context that makes them both understandable and forgivable. This is a request for the reader's sympathy well motivated by the broader movements of the novel. The difficulty raised by Rosamond has to do with *her* relationship to the surrounding social context, the connection between her weaknesses and general social pressures, the link between her character and her education. We are never to forget, after all, that Rosamond's social bearing is not a gift of nature, that it is rather her "art to appear natural." Rosamond may be as lovely as a flower, but she is a "flower of Mrs Lemon's school, the chief school in the county, where the teaching included all that was demanded in the accomplished female" (I, 11).

Furthermore, George Eliot makes plain that the narcissism that is so pronounced and unattractive in Rosamond is itself encouraged by the limits governing female experience. "It had not occurred to Lydgate," we read early in their courtship, "that he had been a subject of eager meditation to Rosamond, who had neither any reason for throwing her marriage into distant perspective, nor any pathological studies to divert her mind from that ruminating habit, that inward repetition of looks, words, and phrases, which makes a large part in the lives of most girls" (II, 16). But what is this if not to suggest that Rosamond's egoism is not some unique pathology but is built into the structural conditions of a young woman's life?

Indeed, as various feminist critics have noted, when we appraise the troubled marriage of Rosamond and Lydgate, we cannot simply point to her narcissistic withdrawal without pointing also to the way that Lydgate persistently and systematically excludes her from certain concerns vital to their life together. Still, if it is undoubtedly true that we should hesitate before blaming Rosamond, it is also true that the narrator scarcely hesitates at all. Having duly catalogued all the mitigating circumstances surrounding her behavior, the narrator still engages in a moral critique that is unambiguous and uncompromising.

In *The Madwoman in the Attic* (1979) Gilbert and Gubar make a strong case for Rosamond as a figure of "female rebellion." Rosamond, they write, is the one who "enacts Dorothea's silent anger against a marriage of death"; the one who accepts "her role as a female"; the one who plots and plans like the author herself and who in combination with Dorothea demonstrates "the heroism of sisterhood without patriarchy." All of this is ingenious; some of it is persuasive;

but the fact remains that however strong we make the defense of Rosamond, the narrator has already rejected that defense. As Gilbert and Gubar put it in another context, George Eliot engages in "acts of vengeance against her own characters," and nowhere is the vengeance more conspicuous than in the rendering of Rosamond.

The question is why this should be so, why it is that a novel that gives us everything needed in order to rehabilitate Rosamond refuses that act of generosity. In part, this can be understood in terms of certain attitudes toward social class. It is notable that of the three romances that bring the plot of the novel to a close, the romance of rediscovered yeoman virtue (Fred and Mary) and the romance of high-born aspiration (Dorothea and Will) achieve solid happiness, while the romance of the urban middle class (Lydgate and Rosamond) follows a sharp downward curve. Within the historical vision that guides the narrative, the middle class is the most clearly associated with the fall from coherent social faith, the fall into the unstable realm of money and public opinion. Much as the novel brings past and future into alliance against the present, so it implies that the respectable workers of the land and the noble inheritors of good blood (Caleb Garth and Dorothea Brooke) come into unspoken alliance against the burghers who dominate the town of Middlemarch. As the child of the new bourgeois sensibility, Rosamond is vulnerable to the charges brought against her class.

More fatal than the suspicions toward class, however, are the novel's suspicions toward gender. This point will sound odd: what can it mean to be suspicious toward gender? The beginning of an answer can be given by reintroducing Will Ladislaw, who has been as controversial a figure for the critics as he is for the good citizens of Middlemarch. Ladislaw has been considered too weightless, too faint, too ephemeral to stand as the proper romantic counterweight to Dorothea. Leslie Stephen gave a representative opinion in an early appreciation of the novel. Ladislaw, he writes,

is scarcely more attractive to most masculine readers than the dandified Stephen Guest. He is a dabbler in art and literature; a small journalist, ready to accept employment from silly Mr. Brooke, and apparently liking to lie on a rug in the houses of his friends and flirt with their pretty wives. He certainly shows indifference to money, and behaves himself correctly to Dorothea, though he has fallen in love with her on her honeymoon. He is no doubt an amiable Bohemian. . . and we can believe that Dorothea was quite content with her lot. But that seems to imply that a Theresa of our days has to be content with suckling fools. . .   (*George Eliot*, 1902)

What informs so much of the common recoiling from Will is that he fails to be an impressive man. The question one might ask, only half facetiously, is how he impresses as a woman. In the manuscript George Eliot had written that his "curves of lip and chin were scarcely shaded by hair even of the shaven sort," and in the published novel, Will is referred to as the "slim young fellow with his girl's complexion" (VI, 60). Dorothea defends him as "a creature who entered into every one's feelings, and could take the pressure of their thought instead of urging his own with iron resistance" (V, 50). Will, in other words, is valued as a receptacle for Dorothea's energies, and quite apart from the startling sexual imagery, it is clear that Will – in his various "attitudes of receptivity" (I, 10) – often plays a role that had traditionally been reserved for the heroine of fiction: the role of complement to the protagonist's virtues, relatively passive and distinctly subordinate to the powers of the central narrative figure. As others have stressed, it is Will's descent through "two generations of rebellious women," his "matrilineal genealogy," that determines his most important personal inheritance. Tellingly, at the moment when Dorothea begins to wake into love of Will, she blends his image with the image of his grandmother Julia that survives in a miniature; and if this does not sufficiently confuse the boundaries of gender, we may recall that Julia has been said to have a "masculine" face (III, 28). It seems clear that George Eliot is wilfully *dissolving* a traditional sexual typology; Will Ladislaw takes on traits conventionally associated with women without ceasing to be the leading man of the novel's central romance. When Lydgate describes Will as "rather miscellaneous and *bric-a-brac*," as "a sort of gypsy" (V, 43), he captures the strongly *hybrid* aspect of Will's sexual character.

Dorothea herself, it should be recalled, is consistently

described as unlike other women, "as if she were under a vow
to be different from all other women" (IV, 37). This is not only
a sign of a moral distinction, but also a sexual distinction.
When Lydgate initially feels that she does not view the world
"from the proper feminine angle," he expresses what the
novel always implies: that the prevailing categories of gender
fail to contain Dorothea, who speaks to James Chettam "very
much with the air of a handsome boy" (I, 2) and whose elo-
quence leaves Mr. Brooke's "masculine consciousness . . . in
rather a stammering condition" (IV, 39). Rosamond is the
one who fits enthusiastically into the category assigned to her;
and so while it is undoubtedly true that she accepts her role
as a woman, this seems not a mark of her strength but an important measure of weakness. For George Eliot the acceptance of the prevailing distinction is always a danger and
often a source of misery.

Indeed, the weakness of the marriage of Lydgate and Rosamond is fundamentally due to their mutual willingness to play
out the fate of their gender assignments. The thirty-sixth
chapter of the novel concludes by summarizing one part of the
difficulty: "Lydgate relied much on the psychological difference between what for the sake of variety I will call goose
and gander: especially on the innate submissiveness of the
goose as beautifully corresponding to the strength of the
gander" (IV, 36). This is not mere complacency; it is, in the
case of Lydgate, a fatal error. He misunderstands that the
theory of the goose and gander is the product of a sentimental
mythology, a false scientism, a construction of sexual roles
that is explosively unstable. Critics who dislike Ladislaw tend
to congratulate George Eliot for her portrait of Lydgate who,
in the words of F. R. Leavis, is "real and a man." But this
misses the fact that it is his conventional masculinity that
becomes his misfortune. The narrator accounts for the taints
in his character by remarking that

Lydgate's spots of commonness lay in the complexion of his pre-
judices, which, in spite of noble intention and sympathy, were half
of them such as are found in ordinary men of the world: that distinction of mind which belonged to his intellectual ardour, did not
penetrate his feeling and judgment about furniture, or women, or

the desirability of its being known (without his telling) that he was
better born than other country surgeons.   (II, 15)

Most striking here is the opposition between Lydgate's intellectual ardour which is his claim to eminence and his feelings about women (associated revealingly with furniture and
good breeding). It is just insofar as Lydgate is a sexual being
that he is common; his distinction depends on his transcending the limits of the sexual differentiation. The concept and
the image of "ardour" (often "ardent") are crucial to the
workings of characterization in *Middlemarch*; the term suggests an emotional intensity that is not opposed to morality
or intellection but is rather their animating principle – so
Dorothea is said to yearn for a life "at once rational and ardent" (I, 10). Indeed, Dorothea and Lydgate are the two
characters in whom the term "ardour" takes deep root, and
in both cases it suggests a form of psychological energy that
sublimates sexual energy and that can carry personality
beyond the usual restrictions of gender. Dorothea's ardour
takes her beyond the region of feminine domesticity, much as
Lydgate's ardour lets him escape the commonness of preoccupation with blood, furniture, and women.
   Certainly the ardour that Dorothea and Lydgate share does
not obliterate the sexual distinction between them, but it points
to a shared ground of personality that may help to explain why
two such strong characters experience no romantic friction.
Critics since Henry James have regretted that George Eliot
decided not to bring them closer together; this regret, however,
may confuse the extent to which the novel is rethinking sexual
identity. One might almost say that Lydgate and Dorothea cannot come together in the narrative because they are of the same
kind, almost of the same sex. The emotionally and morally expansive Dorothea – who "had always been giving out ardour"
(II, 22) – requires a receptive complement like Ladislaw to
"take the pressure" of her sensibility. Furthermore, it begins
to appear that Ladislaw provides the same service for Lydgate.
The narrator pointedly remarks that Will "had more comprehension of Lydgate than Rosamond had"; and in their last
meeting together, when both appear in grave distress, Will

clearly plays the part of the sensitive complement: "The two men were pitying each other, but it was only Will who guessed the extent of his companion's trouble. When Lydgate spoke with desperate resignation of going to settle in London and said with a faint smile, 'We shall have you again, old fellow' Will felt inexpressibly mournful, and said nothing" (VIII, 79).

What makes this so dizzying is that George Eliot, having dissolved the old fixities in the typology of gender, proceeds to rearrange the attributes of sexual identity and to assign them to characters in such a way that the lines between masculinity and femininity begin to blur. Dorothea's relation to Will is the most vivid example, but when the novel suggests that Lydgate is a worthy scientist just to the extent that he transcends his common masculinity, then it becomes impossible to determine the gender of his "intellectual ardour." Similar strains on the conventions of gender appear in the romance of Fred and Mary, Fred inclining to be passive, sentimental and submissive, Mary remaining decisive and firm. Gilbert and Gubar have noticed the "effeminacy" of Bulstrode who asks only to be "a vessel. . . consecrated by use." Indeed the only principal character in the book who remains firmly embedded within the traditional configurations of gender is Rosamond who never struggles against the conventions of femininity, aspiring only to epitomize those conventions.

Metamorphosis

What the discussion so far should suggest is the tense struggle within *Middlemarch* to contemplate a new order of experience while preserving the sanctity of the moral tradition. In the spirit of one of the novel's best-known aphorisms the narrator continues to hold that "Life would be no better than candle-light tinsel and daylight rubbish if our spirits were not touched by what has been" (VI, 54). And yet, this historical novel keeps seeking a way to present an advance through history, to suggest a path toward the "growing good of the world," and in this way to escape a slavish devotion to "what has been." In speaking to Dorothea of what he owes his cousin Casaubon, Will Ladislaw accepts the stern necessity of obligation, but he insists that "Obligation may be stretched till it is no better than a brand of slavery stamped on us when we were too young to know its meaning" (IV, 39). And later when Will learns that his mother's family was involved in the same shady business practices that led to Bulstrode's fortune, he writhes under the weight of the past: "It is important to me to have no stain on my birth and connections. And now I find there is a stain which I can't help." Will is said to be in "passionate rebellion against this inherited blot" (VI, 61), with this phrase neatly capturing the conflict between novelty and tradition, freedom and inheritance.

Will's cult of freedom – his impatience with all restraint, including the restraint of vocation – has led to the charge, found twice in *Middlemarch* itself, that he is "dilettantish." In Casaubon's words, Will drifts "without any special object, save the vague purpose of what he calls culture, preparation for he knows not what" (I, 9). Indeed Will *is* a dilettante, but that is only the beginning, not the end, of the question. George Eliot clearly set out to invent a highly sympathetic character, a character central to the workings of her plot, in the guise of a dilettante. Why should this be so? The short answer is that dilettantism is essential to Will's attractions for her and to her reflections on change and growth.

During the early debate over Will's moral laxity, the narrator steps forward to say that "We know what a masquerade all development is, and what effective shapes may be disguised in helpless embryos. – In fact, the world is full of hopeful analogies and handsome dubious eggs called possibilities" (I, 10). The talk of embryo and egg is enough to bring Darwin back into focus, and indeed the career of Will Ladislaw contains the novel's most serious use of Darwinian insight into the understanding of character within history. The strange twists of human development, the confusing passage from egg to chick, from possibility to actuality – these are some of the issues that preoccupied George Eliot most deeply and that she came to understand through the work of Darwin, especially Darwin as passed through the exposition of George Henry Lewes. In one of his *Fortnightly Review* essays on Darwin in 1868 ("Mr. Darwin's Hypotheses"), Lewes describes the "marvel of marvels" as the fact that an exceedingly minute portion of living matter, so simple in structure that a line will define it, passes by successive modifications into an organism so complex that a treatise is needed to describe it. . . A microscopic cell of albuminous compounds, wholly without trace of organs, not appreciably distinguishable from millions of other cells, does nevertheless contain within it the "possibilities" of an organism so complex and so special as that of a Newton or a Napoleon.

Part of what George Eliot is studying in both Will and Dorothea is this marvellous passage from cell to character. But even more ambitious than the reflection on individual development is the reflection on the development of the species. James Chettam identifies Will as "volatile" and "unriveted," and though Chettam is suspect, his judgment here is not. Will's most important trait is his ability to vary his traits. In an illuminating early description the narrator speaks of "the uncertainty of his changing expression. Surely, his very features changed their form; his jaw looked sometimes large and sometimes small; and the little ripple in his nose was a preparation for metamorphosis" (II, 21). This last phrase puts the point definitively − Will in "preparation for metamorphosis" is the novel's embodiment of Darwin's epoch-making insight into the evolution of the organism. That the fixity of species is a myth, that organisms vary, and that complex animals invariably develop from less complex animals − these were bitterly debated principles that George Eliot brought into her novel, most particularly through the figure of Ladislaw. What makes Will Ladislaw such a difficult character for readers is that he is the product of the novel's most strenuous attempt to reveal human character as "a process and an unfolding." Because he incarnates the perception that the experience of the species, like the experience of the self, is a becoming not a mere being, he eludes the grasp of the reader who is accustomed to know (at the very least) whether a given jaw is large or small.

Still, Will's susceptibility to change cannot be at the expense of his entanglement in tradition. There is the inherited blot of his family's immorality; there is the special link to his grandmother Julia; and more subtly and comically there is his relationship to Mr. Brooke. The connection between

Brooke and Ladislaw – Brooke as the fond and foolish patron, Ladislaw as the gifted and impatient protégé – will seem odd until it is realized how much they share. Brooke's chief trait and leading mannerism is his proud claim that he "took in all the new ideas at one time" (I, 2), and that he has "gone into everything." It is Brooke's accurate perception that Will was "at home in all those artistic and literary subjects which Mr. Brooke had gone into at one time" (IV, 37). Brooke, in brief, is another dilettante, but it would be facile merely to identify the two characters, without recognizing that George Eliot carefully places them in a developmental – evolutionary – line. As Lewes puts the Darwinian claim, "There is not a single known example of an organism which is not developed out of simpler forms." Mr. Brooke is that simpler form out of which Ladislaw develops; in their relationship the process of evolution stands exposed.

This is especially so in the part of the plot that gives most explicit attention to the drama of political reform. Having hired Ladislaw to manage his journal *The Pioneer*, Brooke has recruited an ally in his reforming campaign. In the event, Brooke shows himself to be erratic, unprepared, silly, and ineffective; his reformist impulses struggle unsuccessfully against the habits of a complacent landowner. Brooke, in effect, represents a premature, unevolved historical possibility; but if he is premature, Will Ladislaw is right on time. After listening to Brooke's mass of contradictory opinions, simultaneously for and against reform, Will insists on the need to respond to the changing demands of social life. Brooke listens obligingly, and then says "You'd never get elected, you know." But of course, as we learn in the "Finale," Will does get elected. Lydgate says harshly of Brooke that "He's not fit to be a public man" (V, 46), and the phrase echoes in the novel's last pages, when Will is described precisely as an "ardent public man" ("Finale"). A fit has at last been found.

The idea of "fitness," with all its Darwinian resonances, is crucial to the book's understanding of history. In the language of Lewes' biology, the issue concerns the adaptation of an Organism to its Medium; in *Middlemarch* the preferred formulation is Character and Environment or, more conventionally, Self and Society. In whatever terms the relationship is cast, the decisive question is a question of fit. Lydgate appears as a distinct evolutionary advance over Casaubon; of the two seekers after knowledge, Lydgate is the one who understands that metaphysical speculation must give way to the rigors of science. But it is part of George Eliot's own rigor to keep her "scientific phoenix" (VII, 63) from triumph, to show on the contrary that even the necessary development from metaphysics to science must contend with the impurities of the social environment. Lydgate is an organism ill-matched with its medium, an organism moreover with its own defects and impurities but too proud to bend to the needs of circumstance.

Ladislaw, on the other hand, is essentially "receptive," and "responsive." "If you go in for the principle of Reform," he tells Brooke, "you must be prepared to take what the situation offers" (V, 46). The principle here goes well beyond the political domain. Taking what the situation offers as one pursues the cause of reform – this is the novel's Darwinian justification of the dilettante. As Dorothea well realizes in her early defense of Will, "people may really have in them some vocation which is not quite plain to themselves, may they not? They may seem idle and weak because they are growing" (I, 9). The free play in Will's life as a dilettante is the freedom to accept metamorphosis until its work is done, until a vocation is uncovered which can adjust to the demands of the social medium without compromising its integrity. It has often been supposed that the final departure of Will from Middlemarch is a sign of his *failure* to adapt to the medium. On the contrary, it is a sign that the medium is changing as well as the organism. The novel's sense of history confirms Will's own view that "political writing, political speaking, would get a higher value now public life was going to be wider and more national" (V, 51). The move from Middlemarch is a move from an obsolete provincialism toward the more contemporary participation in national community. The organism has changed; the medium has changed. Will has metamorphosed from poetry to politics, by way of his love for Dorothea, and public life has evolved from the province to the nation. The result is that *Middlemarch* shows not only (through Lydgate) how the struggle for existence has tragic consequences but also (through Will) how it can end in the happy marriage of organism and medium.

Life in time

As the novel's re-visions of gender brought us inevitably to its more general treatment of metamorphosis, so metamorphosis forces us back to the question of life in time, where this is now not simply a matter of public historical time, the time of political reform or medical revolution, but rather the time of immediate experience, what might be called *the temporality of ordinary life*. To live in the world for George Eliot is necessarily to take up an attitude toward the movement of time; it is to have a *temporal disposition*, a posture and a bearing toward time that shows itself in our most immediate experiences of memory, anticipation, regret, hope, expectation. Because there are many ways to have (or to refuse to have) these experiences, there are many ways to live in time, and it is a central project in *Middlemarch* to distinguish these ways in order to distinguish the good life from the bad, and to distinguish both of these from the indifferent.

Early in the novel, when Dorothea happily projects her life as Casaubon's wife, she imagines reading Latin and Greek to him "as Milton's daughters did to their father" (I, 7). Then late in the book, when she believes that Will Ladislaw loves Rosamond and so suffers at the thought of her loss, she forms an image of the Will she has loved and the Will who has betrayed her:

There were two images -- two living forms that tore her heart in two, as if it had been the heart of a mother who seems to see her child divided by the sword, and presses one bleeding half to her breast while her gaze goes forth in agony towards the half which is carried away by the lying woman that has never known the mother's pang.
(VIII, 80)

This is a highly startling conceit, startling in its violence and startling in the role that Dorothea pictures for herself. Since Will has been associated with a variety of Romantic poets,

principal among them Shelley, we could say that Dorothea
has passed from wanting to be Milton's daughter to wanting
to be Shelley's mother. Here is one instance of George Eliot's
demanding notion of life in time. Dorothea, it appears, can
only become a wife after she has trained herself to be a
daughter and a mother. Put in the more abstract way that the
novel also encourages, the suggestion is that a full life in the
present is only possible in the context of authentic relations
to past and future, "authentic" in a sense that should become
clearer as we proceed.

What makes Dorothea's attitudes so impressive an accomplishment is that George Eliot's works contain a virtual
lexicon of the various *inauthentic* relations to time. To take
just one pertinent example from another novel, Godfrey Cass
in *Silas Marner* finds himself in a romantic crisis and a financial crisis, and faced with these difficulties, "He fled to his
usual refuge, that of hoping for some unforeseen turn of fortune, some favourable chance which would save him from
unpleasant consequences. . . . Favourable Chance is the god
of all men who follow their own devices instead of obeying
a law they believe in" (I, 9). Within *Middlemarch* Lydgate is
the one who faces the romantic and monetary troubles
anticipated by Godfrey Cass, and in his desperation he turns
briefly to gambling, guided by the bitter perception that
"chance has an empire which reduces choice to a fool's illusion" (VII, 64).

What Chance becomes to Lydgate, Providence has always
been to Bulstrode: the refuge from the heavy weight of
responsibility. If Bulstrode grows rich at the expense of
others, if this spiritual pride is purchased by sordid profits,
if he allows his housekeeper to send Raffles toward death,
this is the will of Providence that allows Bulstrode to rationalize his desires. A trust in Providence is for George Eliot
as self-deceptive and as pernicious as a faith in Chance. Both
are essentially magical attempts to solve the problem of Time,
by relying on a mythical deity independent of the will. They
are attempts to escape the responsibility for *acknowledging*
the past and *constructing* the future by regarding the movement of time as the work of odds or Gods.

To the terrible dyad, Chance and Providence, a third term needs to be added. The term is Romance, and it has its fullest realization in the career of Rosamond Vincy, whose first brief encounters with Lydgate become for her "the opening incidents of a preconceived romance — incidents which gather value from the foreseen development and climax" (II, 16). The "preconceptions" of Romance are what George Eliot likes least in it, the fantasy of an entirely foreseen triumph that is based on nothing more than "a group of airy conditions" (VII, 64). When her marriage to Lydgate falls into a mutual estrangement that is anything but romantic, Rosamond keeps alive her restless fantasy by imagining that Will Ladislaw would have made "a much more suitable husband for her than she had found in Lydgate" — to which thought the narrator responds with detectable anger:

No notion could have been falser than this, for Rosamond's discontent in her marriage was due to the conditions of marriage itself, to its demand for self-suppression and tolerance, and not to the nature of her husband; but the easy conception of an unreal Better had a sentimental charm which diverted her ennui. She constructed a little romance which was to vary the flatness of her life. . .   (VIII,75)

"The easy conception of an unreal Better" — this is what Chance, Providence and Romance share, the lazy desire to pretend that time will take care of itself and that the future is not of our making.

There is, however, another aspect of Rosamond that points to another aspect of the novel's presentation of life in time. Because if Rosamond is a fantasist, she is also a scientist in the service of her fantasies. "No one [was] quicker than Rosamond to see causes and effects which lay within the track of her own tastes and interests" (VI, 58). If she is depicted as wholly unconcerned with an honest appraisal of the conditions of her life, she is also depicted — this is part of the narrator's cold fury directed at her — as intensely calculating in pursuit of her private satisfactions. Here is the antithetical evil to the abdication of choice: the fierce egoistic insistence on choosing an agreeable future. As with Rosamond's Romance, so with Bulstrode's Providence: it too acts to convert abstention of the will into a useful instrument for willful

desires. Indeed much of the plot turns on the contents of
wills, now in the sense of legal documents disposing property,
as in the cases of Featherstone and Casaubon. It is clear that
in the perverse stipulations of their respective wills –
Featherstone's savage disappointment of the expectations of
his legal kin, including Fred Vincy, and Casaubon's offensive
codicil withdrawing the property from Dorothea if she marries
Ladislaw – both characters exemplify the more general
dangers associated with will in the psychological sense: the
will as the grasping instrument of an ego intent to control the
future.

After he listens to the reading of Featherstone's will, Caleb
Garth says, "For my part, I wish there was no such thing as
a will" (IV, 35). When the opinion is immediately challenged
as un-Christian, Garth makes no defense, but it is clear that
George Eliot shares a deep suspicion of the desire to direct the
movement of time with a "dead hand" tightly gripping the
future. But here is a deep difficulty. For if one relinquishes
the will to master time, with all its suggestions of tight egoistic
control, isn't the alternative then the flight from choice and
responsibility, the retreat into the imaginary refuge of gambling,
or romantic fantasy, or religious superstition? Is there any
place to stand between self-abdication and self-will?

Caleb Garth is central to the novel's struggle with these
questions, especially in his dispute with his wife over the marriage of Fred and Mary. Susan Garth, who cherishes hopes
that Farebrother will marry her daughter, is bitterly sceptical
toward Fred's prospects. Still, when Caleb insists on helping
Fred to become a better man, she affectionately gives way.

But she went out and had a hearty cry to make up for the suppression
of her words. She felt sure that her husband's conduct would be
misunderstood, and about Fred she was rational and unhopeful.
Which would turn out to have the more foresight in it – her rationality
or Caleb's ardent generosity?   (VI, 56)

Just to formulate the question in this way is already to in-
dicate what answer the novel will give: indeed, Caleb's ardent
generosity does prove to have more foresight than Susan's
rationality. This crucial exchange must be seen as George

Eliot's attempt to distinguish herself from the rationalism that is a permanent temptation within her aesthetic. Susan Garth is a rational realist, honest and courageous, and in pointing to the limitations of her view, the novel points to the limits of George Eliot's original understanding of the realist project. The passage aims then toward an alternative to realism that is also an alternative way of being in time.

In this respect the naming of Susan Garth's rationality as "unhopeful" is highly significant, and it becomes more significant still when one recalls that "hopeful" is precisely the epithet that summarizes Fred Vincy's character. From his introduction to his parting bow, Fred is described as "hopeful." His hopefulness is carefully distinguished from (though also closely related to) the fantasies of Rosamond and the self-deceptions of Bulstrode. When Fred's instinctive hopefulness turns into "expectation," when he builds his fantasies of receiving the home and the wealth of the dying Featherstone, he comes close to his sister in his approach to the easy refuge of an "unreal Better." But when Featherstone's will shatters his fantasies, then he gains the opportunity to remake his moral world by reorienting himself in time. His chance lies not in becoming, like Susan Garth, "rational and unhopeful," but in keeping his hopes from degenerating into expectations. Hope without expectation – this is the delicately poised temporal condition that the novel attempts to render, a generous opening toward the future that must always resist clasping its hands around imaginary entitlements.

It is Dorothea who brings this difficult condition to its fullest realization. In the early pages of *Middlemarch* Dorothea shows herself to be another eager young fantasist, imagining the "grand life" she could lead as Casaubon's wife, but no sooner has she begun to spin the romantic web, then she "check[s] herself suddenly with self-rebuke for the presumptuous way in which she was reckoning on uncertain events" (I, 3). As the novel unfolds and as even her abbreviated fantasy is cruelly destroyed, Dorothea withdraws ever further from projections into the time to come. Lydgate says of her admiringly that "She evidently thinks nothing of

her own future" (VIII, 76); and just a few pages later the narrator observes of her relation to Will Ladislaw that "She
entertained no visions of their ever coming into nearer union,
and yet she had taken no posture of renunciation" (VIII, 77).
This puts the issue in compelling and difficult terms:
Dorothea cultivates no visions of happiness; neither does she
renounce happiness. In characteristically uncompromising
fashion, George Eliot asks her protagonist to relinquish a
view of the future as subject to knowledge and control, to
give up the idea of imagining any determinate content for the
future – to do this, however, without surrendering responsibility for the future that we are not permitted to foresee.

The largest implications of this personal bearing emerge in
Dorothea's central statement of her faith, part of which was
quoted earlier. Will has called her life "a dreadful imprison-
ment"; she has said that she has "no longings." The scene
then continues in this way.

He did not speak, but she replied to some change in his expression.
"I mean, for myself. Except that I should like not to have so much
more than my share without doing anything for others. But I have
a belief of my own, and it comforts me."
"What is that?" said Will, rather jealous of the belief.
"That by desiring what is perfectly good, even when we don't
quite know what it is and cannot do what we would, we are part of
the divine power against evil – widening the skirts of light and making
the struggle with darkness narrower."   (IV, 39)

This obligation to do good without knowing in what the good
consists – this is the moral call that is voiced all through
Middlemarch and that makes it such a poignantly pleading,
poignantly uncertain appeal. We cannot know the good; we
can only that know the good is what we must serve – that is
our enervating condition at this moment in moral history.

Love in time

To show the tight solidarity among some apparently distinct
concerns of *Middlemarch* – the problems of gender, of
metamorphosis, of life in time – has been one of the chief
aims of this chapter. But the relationship among these

concerns cannot become perspicuous until a further question is posed, the question of love.

At the center of *Middlemarch* stands a chapter called "Three Love Problems," the title itself suggesting both that love itself can become a problem and that it is a problem in more than one way. The previous chapter had taught that "There are many wonderful mixtures in the world which are all alike called love" (III, 31), and this, we now recognize, is part of the essential teaching of the novel. Our nomenclature blinds us to reality; names disguise the diversity of experience, implying as they do that signs correspond to single referents, whereas in fact one sign must undergo ceaseless variation: "Signs are small measurable things, but interpretations are illimitable" (I, 3). "Love" poses special difficulties, because it has been made into a magical sign used to validate many strange "mixtures," and one of the responsibilities assumed by *Middlemarch* is to disentangle the varieties of love from the magic of its name.

What makes this a special problem for *Middlemarch* is that love is not simply a problem for its characters but a problem for its author. George Eliot's commitment to the moral sense is so unyielding, and within that commitment her sanctification of duty is so uncompromising, that love risks disappearing as a high value. Dorothea's early decision to marry Casaubon epitomizes the difficulty. In the yearning for a high moral mission, love simply drops out of account. Henceforth, a struggle of the narrative is how to recover a place for love within a revised understanding of morality itself.

It is, of course, in the marriage of Rosamond and Lydgate that the dangers of love are most vividly dramatized. Of the "three love problems," theirs is the most disruptive to the novel's search for moral equanimity, and in trying to explain this further, one might point to its dangerous conjunction of passionate instinct and social artifice. Lydgate possesses the "power of passionate love" (III, 31), an attribute conspicuously displayed in the tale of his obsession with the actress Laure. Rosamond, on the other hand, is "not one of those helpless girls who betray themselves unawares, and whose behaviour is awkwardly driven by their impulses" (III, 27);

she coolly guides herself by the norms of correctness and social grace. Her cool propriety and his warm emotion are both insufficient. They are equally distant from the conscious act of sympathy that for George Eliot gives the only secure foundation for love, just as it gives the only firm basis for morality.

What complicates this picture further, and what moves it from satire toward tragedy, is that the contrast between artifice and instinct, exquisite self-control and impulsive emotion, overlays a still deeper contrast. Rosamond may be the consummate embodiment of a socially fashioned identity, but *Middlemarch* makes unmistakably plain that her social aspiration emanates from biological sources. Her unrelenting egoism places her close to the animal kingdom apparently so remote from the drawing-room. The relationship between Rosamond and Lydgate, so demurely begun, descends inexorably into violence. The biology that underlies sociology invites the novel into several startling conceits, as for instance when Rosamond's conviction that they are "as good as engaged" struggles with Lydgate's "counter-idea." We then learn that

Circumstance was almost sure to be on the side of Rosamond's idea, which had a shaping activity and looked through watchful blue eyes, whereas Lydgate's lay blind and unconcerned as a jelly-fish which gets melted without knowing it.   (III, 27)

This prepares for the pathology of love, love reduced to a contest of wills with nothing distinctively human about their competition. George Eliot is not content to display a failure of human intimacy, to establish the "total missing of each other's mental track" so devastating in this marriage; she aims to the still more awful thought, that human beings can be so essentially opposing in their interests, desires and aims that it is for all the world as if they were "creatures of different species" (VI, 58).

Lydgate and especially Rosamond, we have seen, are the two characters most comfortably situated within the prevailing categories of gender. The narrator tells us that Rosamond possesses all that was wanted in an "accomplished female";

and Lydgate, to recall Leavis, is "real and a man." The troubling implication, then, is that insofar as these two meet the conventional expectations of human love, they risk the terrible descent into animal cruelty: Lydgate "wanted to smash and grind some object on which he could at least produce an impression, or else to tell her brutally that he was master, and she must obey" (VII, 64). Their form of love is an invitation to regression. It is a reminder that human beings always remain susceptible to the amoral imperatives of their biology.

Among the uses to which the romance of Fred Vincy and Mary Garth is put, one of the most important is to offer a critique of the Rosamond/Lydgate romance. Much as Caleb Garth becomes a sign for an organic tradition jeopardized by the modernizing nineteenth century, so Fred and Mary come to signify a newly threatened tradition of love. Lydgate appears to Rosamond as an exotic stranger to Middlemarch traditions, and "a stranger was absolutely necessary to Rosamond's social romance" (I, 12). The craving for a future full of novelty, an indulgence that George Eliot sees as a mark of decadence, is sharply contrasted in the bond between Fred and Mary, which celebrates time past. The leading characteristic of their love is that it is an ancient love, an old, old passion dating from their earliest consciousness.

"I have never been without loving Mary," says Fred, "If I had to give her up, it would be like beginning to live on wooden legs" (V, 52). Mary, for her part, explains to her father that it is not because Fred is a fine match that she loves him. "What for, then?" asks Caleb. "Oh dear," she answers, "because I have always loved him." Any break in their companionship "would make too great a difference to us — like seeing all the old places altered, and changing the name for everything" (VIII, 86). These are the conceits George Eliot favors; the failure of human love would not be simply a frustrating of instinctive desire; it would be a change in the contours of experience. It would be as if all had changed, one's body, one's world, one's language.

What gives special force to this picture of fidelity in *Middlemarch* is that the novel indeed offers a more fit match for

Mary Garth, in the person of the Reverend Camden Farebrother. All concerned see that Farebrother is the better man and see further that he could love and be loved by Mary Garth. It is when Mary herself sees this that the novel gives its most studied reflection on the virtues of constancy. Through Fred's sulky jealousy Mary is made to contemplate the thought of Farebrother marrying her, and in response she braces herself to keep her desires as they have always been. The narrator elaborates:

When a tender affection has been storing itself in us through many of our years, the idea that we could accept any exchange for it seems to be a cheapening of our lives. And we can set a watch over our affections and our constancy as we can over other treasures.(VI, 57)

This view can be regarded as the official moral position in George Eliot's fiction, a secure belief in the solidarity between love and duty. Human desire, though dangerously unstable, can be controlled through acts of moral attention, can be trained and tutored, can be directed to its proper end: the cherishing of old commitments. The coherence of the world and the integrity of the self depend on gestures of deliberate emotional preservation. Here, in her most conservative aspect, George Eliot understands love as a confirming of the already loved ("because I have always loved him"), as an ongoing reassertion of emotional identity through time, as a conscious embrace of continuity.

The final conversation between Mary and her father, in which she affirms her abiding love for Fred, enjoys the privilege of being the last scene in the novel before its "Finale." George Eliot had not originally intended it for this spot, but her decision to move it there may well reflect an eagerness to lend it more weight within the novel's scale of values. Set against it stands the provocation of the love between Dorothea and Will, which represents a difficult challenge to the pastoral simplicity of what one might call Garthian love.

Unlike Mary, Dorothea does not bring ancient love to her future husband. On the contrary, as the stammering Mr. Brooke explains to the enraged James Chettam, the engagement has "come about quite suddenly – neither of them had any idea two days ago – not any idea, you know. There's something singular in things" (VIII, 84). "Singular" is apt. The romance between Dorothea and Will stands out as an exotic exception, not only to the settled conservatism of love among the Garths, but to the narrow preferences of the Middlemarch community, as well as to some of George Eliot's own deep predilections. When Celia complains to her sister that "you *said* you would never be married again" (VIII, 84), Dorothea has no rejoinder. She has broken a private vow and has departed from a firm conviction. What has happened to those dignified virtues of self-identity, constancy of desire, continuity of emotion?

To answer most simply, what has happened is Casaubon's will. When Dorothea learns that her husband has had such shameful thoughts of her association with Will Ladislaw, she suffers a break in the continuity of her world, a break that cannot be repaired.

She might have compared her experience at that moment to the vague, alarmed consciousness that her life was taking on a new form, that she was undergoing a metamorphosis in which memory would not adjust itself to the stirring of new organs. Everything was changing its aspect: her husband's conduct, her own duteous feeling towards him, every struggle between them – and yet more, her whole relation to Will Ladislaw. Her world was in a state of convulsive change; the only thing she could say distinctly to herself was, that she must wait and think anew. One change terrified her as if it had been a sin; it was a violent shock of repulsion from her departed husband, who had had hidden thoughts, perhaps perverting everything she said and did. Then again she was conscious of another change which also made her tremulous; it was a sudden strange yearning of heart towards Will Ladislaw. (V, 50)

Not the reassurance of continuity and tradition, but the violence of "convulsive change" – this is the condition of Dorothea's first turn of heart toward Will. The passage makes clear, ironically, caustically, that Casaubon has made possible the very circumstance he sought to prevent, Dorothea's "yearning" for Will. Crucial to George Eliot's understanding of this new emotion is that it is the product of "metamorphosis," and here we rejoin a previous concern. For despite all her temperamental desire to preserve the organic past, George Eliot had accepted the Darwinian insight that an organism may have a strange career.

Well-established now, as the narrator has told us, is the notion that many "mixtures" have been called by the name of "love." The craving for novelty that characterizes Rosamond's "thin romance" is sharply rebuked in Mary Garth's firm affective constancy. But that constancy is itself implicitly challenged by the "metamorphosis" that changes Dorothea's world and allows her to move toward Will. *Middlemarch* is intent to think past the pieties of Garthian love in order to ask how the idea of reform − certainly the central idea in this historical novel − applies to the life of desires as well as to the political life.

The romance of Lydgate and Rosamond is an instance of false novelty, a mere fantasy of the new aroused by luscious ruminations on the future. Dorothea, we recall, "thinks nothing of her own future." It is at the moment when Dorothea most thoroughly abandons hope of a romantic tie with Will that the romance becomes a reality. A bright future appears to her only when she has utterly abandoned any expectations of future happiness, when, like Rosamond under her own moral influence, she "ceased thinking how anything would turn out − merely wondering what would come" (VIII, 81). Dorothea is *surprised* by love, and it is clear that the capacity for surprise is essential to George Eliot's view of the good life. We must exist in a state of moral readiness, without thinking how things will turn out, not relying on the beneficence of the future but ready to be surprised by it.

When after the revelation of Casaubon's will Dorothea has what she assumes to be a final parting from Ladislaw, she experiences a new emotion that she cannot yet identify: "She did not know then that it was Love who had come to her briefly, as in a dream before awaking, with the hues of morning on his wings − that it was Love to whom she was sobbing her farewell as his image was banished by the blameless rigour of irresistible day" (VI, 55). How like George Eliot to begin a sentence with a paean to Love and to end with the rigour of the irresistible; and how like Dorothea to inhabit the world that such a sentence describes. It would not be too much to say that, in its private domain, the work of the novel is to establish a solidarity between the two halves of the sentence and to create a condition in which love and rigour can flourish together.

The terrible fate of Rosamond and Lydgate is to fall toward the endless competition of interests that marks them as "creatures of different species." In their first encounters it would seem that Will and Dorothea are similarly distinct creatures, he with his cult of sensations, she with her shrine to duty. But their marriage is the marriage of two metamorphs, whose greatest claim in this novel of reform is that they are form changers, concept subverters, mutants. Will, we learn, is "made of very impressible stuff. The bow of a violin drawn near him cleverly, would at one stroke change the aspect of the world for him, and his point of view shifted as easily as his mood" (IV, 39). Dorothea is not nearly so "impressible," but she too, and crucially, is capable of shifting her point of view and changing the aspect of her world. The ability to experience a fundamental reform of self is what separates these two from Lydgate and Rosamond quite as firmly as from Mary and Fred. One might mention in passing that it separates them equally from Bulstrode, whose experiences might, after all, have led to moral metamorphosis. But even after his reputation has been shattered and no dignity remains to be preserved, Bulstrode is incapable of confessing his crime to his wife: "concealment had been the habit of his life, and the impulse to confession had no power against the dread of a deeper humiliation" (VIII, 85).

This chapter began by arguing that one of the great challenges posed by *Middlemarch* is directed at prevailing categories of gender, and now it can end by remarking that the attack on categories extends still more widely, until it unsettles the distinction between art and morality which had seemed so fundamental at its start. Will enters the novel as the aesthete, Dorothea as the moralist. But by the time they exchange their passionate kiss, they have not only ceased to be the usual representatives of masculine and feminine, but also the representatives of art and morality. Will becomes the politicized aesthete, Dorothea the amorous moralist.

And yet a revealing asymmetry remains in these two trans-formations, an asymmetry that bears on the discouragement felt by many contemporary readers. Will journeys from aestheticism to moral earnestness, while Dorothea, who had epitomized earnest morality, moves not to art but to love. So many details of George Eliot's own early life enter into the portrait of Dorothea Brooke that the possibility of authorship is conspicuous by its absence. Dorothea learns to love but not to narrate. She must content herself with an unknown, unremembered benevolence rather than the power of cultural eminence enjoyed by her creator. This novel, so preoccupied with the problem of vocation, remains silent on the vocation of novelist, and in keeping that silence it preserves an un-bridgeable gap between author and character. Why? Perhaps because George Eliot could not shake the cold perception that while moral virtue is rare indeed, literary genius is still rarer.

Chapter 5

The afterlife of a masterpiece

Middlemarch, we know, is a novel acutely conscious of the problem of reputation. From Rosamond's habit of always considering the "audience in her own consciousness" to Casaubon's desperate worry over the reception of his *magnum opus*, from Dorothea's sad submission to the unflattering views of "common eyes" to Bulstrode's humiliation before the townspeople, from Lydgate's quickly rising reputation to its sudden spirit-killing fall, the novel is preoccupied with the awful powers of repute. In a significant sense already considered, the novel is about the force of public opinion. All the principal characters in the work must come to recognize the frightening strength of this social god.

The scandal of her "marriage" to Lewes would have been enough to make George Eliot sensitive to the issue, but as Alexander Welsh (1985) has convincingly shown, the concern with reputation – and especially the fear of blackmail which recurs in George Eliot's fiction – can be linked to the development of a society organized around the exchange of information, a society which produces more opinions much as it produces more goods. No doubt both her private life and the changing public world led George Eliot to think hard about the stresses of reputation; it is clear that even in the throes of her great fame, she wondered about the effect of her novels on that great hazy amorphous entity, the Popular Mind. And just as she was beginning *Middlemarch* she wrote to a correspondent that she was "beginning to see with new clearness, that if a book which has any sort of exquisiteness happens also to be a popular widely circulated book, its power over the social mind, for any good, is after all due to its reception by a few appreciative natures, and it is the slow result of radiation from that narrow circle." Her hope for her novel thus resembles her hope for Dorothea Brooke: that a steadily widening influence might at last make a difference in the world.

This is a noble view, but it has little connection with the history of *Middlemarch*'s reputation, which has been anything but a steady extension of the ever-broadening circle and which has instead resembled the erratic courses traced by the reputations of a Bulstrode or a Lydgate. The initial response to the novel was overwhelmingly favorable, leading, as Gordon S. Haight (1968) has put it, to a "crescendo of fame" for its author. The reviewer for *The Daily Telegraph* wrote that it would be "almost profane to speak of ordinary novels in the same breath with George Eliot's." "What do I think of Middlemarch?" wrote Emily Dickinson and then added, "What do I think of glory?" It would be easy to multiply examples such as this. There are countless anecdotes of the way *Middlemarch* came suddenly to pervade the English-speaking readership.

It is one sign of the preeminence George Eliot achieved through *Middlemarch* that, when a year after its publication Thomas Hardy began to serialize *Far From the Madding Crowd*, the work was immediately taken for her newest fiction. Then, after its author was known, Hardy could take little cheer: the reviews of the novel complained that it was far too derivative. This is unfair. Hardy occupies his own place in the late nineteenth-century history of the novel; but it is a measure of George Eliot's massive presence on the contemporary scene that she could so easily be thought to absorb Hardy's novelty. Certainly it is true that as a "study of provincial life" *Middlemarch* authoritatively confirmed the dignity of the literary regionalism that George Eliot had pursued since the beginning of her career and that she successfully established as a counterweight to the metropolis of Dickens. Hardy mocked that George Eliot had no direct knowledge of life in the fields, but it is evident that her monumental study of provincial life gave him a broad highway out of London.

Hardy correctly recognized the author of *Middlemarch* as an obstacle in his way, a large presence that jeopardized his originality. Indeed, George Moore (1921) spoke of Hardy as "one of George Eliot's miscarriages," and though the phrase is as unjust as it is cruel, it does remind us of her literary maternity. Even in such distinctive aspects of Hardy's work as his representation of modern tragedy, George Eliot leaves traces of her ancestry. The fatality of chance, the frailty of the self when faced with the blind powers of circumstance, the relative poverty of the moral will – these are intensifications, albeit to the point of originality, of the perception of the necessity that so often appears in *Middlemarch*.

To say this is only to validate the perception of George Eliot's contemporaries who so often regretted what they saw as the downward emotional drift of the novel. As Patrick Swinden (1972) has pointed out, a recurrent late-Victorian theme was the complaint that the novel was so "melancholy": so for instance the reviewer for the *Spectator* sighed that "George Eliot never makes the world worse than it is, but she makes it a shade darker." And Sidney Colvin, writing in the *Fortnightly Review* (1873) wondered whether a large and ambitious work of literature such as *Middlemarch* is obliged "like life itself, to leave us sad and hungry" – to which one might properly respond that this is no more conclusive an interpretation of *Middlemarch* than it is of life.

Middlemarch itself avoids the dominance of the tragic tone; indeed, one of the characteristics most responsible for the sharply winding course of its historical reception is that it so carefully adjusts its balance of tones and modes. The note of tragic compulsion fades into a note of romantic liberation, the large symphonic amplitude keeping any tone from becoming final. In accounting for the diverse early response to the novel, one must look, for instance, at the large body of fiction inspired by the so-called New Woman in the eighties and nineties, the work of writers such as Grant Allan, Ella Hepworth Dixon and Mary Cholmondeley. Dorothea Brooke, in her willingness to disregard the pieties of common moral wisdom and to risk moral exile, unquestionably stands as an early avatar of the New Woman. When she stoutly resists Mrs. Cadwallader's conventionalism by insisting that "the greater part of the world is mistaken about many things" (VI, 54), she prepares for the wave of late nineteenth-century women, fictive and real, who challenge the orthodoxy of the age, especially the marital orthodoxy. And yet, of course, Dorothea's rebellion is kept carefully in check; she is in embryo a figure of the revolutionary "woman who did," but only in embryo. *Middlemarch*, one might say, remains equidistant from Hardy's tragic novels and the liberationist fiction of the New Woman — equidistant while preparing the foundations for both.

Of all George Eliot's immediate successors, Henry James is the one most intent to grant her eminence and then to square accounts with her. Through much of James's career he conducted an agitated dialogue with her, his ambivalences well reflected in the opening line of his 1873 review: *Middlemarch* "is at once one of the strongest and one of the weakest of English novels." Where it is strong is in its remarkable imaginative reach, in its creation of "a picture — vast, swarming, deep-coloured, crowded with episodes, with vivid images, with lurking master-strokes, with brilliant passages of expression; and as such we may freely accept it and enjoy it." As only the greatest novels can do, it creates a "supreme sense of the vastness and variety of human life." What is more, its imaginative density is accompanied by the "constant presence of thought, of generalizing instinct, of *brain*," a conviction of intellectual seriousness that James saw as the urgent precondition of progress beyond "the old-fashioned English novel." That he felt George Eliot as an illustrious ally in the reform of fiction is not only evident in his critical endorsement but also in his imaginative solidarity. It is now well established that James's *The Portrait of a Lady* (1883) owes many of its particular details (for instance, the evocation of Rome) and much of its general conception (especially the conception of Isabel Archer herself) directly to the example of *Middlemarch*.

James often took a hearty and generous delight in the achievement of his own most important English predecessor. But from his earliest review, this delight sits close beside some pointed and highly influential criticism. Even in the midst of his high praise James regrets the failure of *Middlemarch* to become "an organized, moulded, balanced composition, gratifying the reader with a sense of design and construction." The novel strikes him as a collection of episodes ungoverned by any superintending plan: in James's famous phrase, "*Middlemarch* is a treasure-house of details, but it is an indifferent whole."

What makes this line of criticism so prescient is that thirty years later, when the century turned and when another generation began to consolidate its anti-Victorian novelistic principles, arguments like those James directed against *Middlemarch* would become dominant. The primacy of narrative form, the great value of unity, the importance of precise compositional design — James, more than anyone else, brought these aesthetic virtues toward supremacy, and from the standpoint of those virtues, *Middlemarch* was full of vice. In his early review of the novel Sidney Colvin (1873) had remarked, in an apt phrase, that what George Eliot writes is "full of her time." *Middlemarch* is

saturated with modern ideas and poured into a language of which every word bites home with peculiar sharpness to the contemporary consciousness. That is what makes it less safe than it might seem at first sight to speak for posterity in such a case. We are afraid of exaggerating the meaning such a work will have for those who come after us, for the very reason that we feel its meaning so pregnant for ourselves.

Indeed, in the half century that followed *Middlemarch* the aura of the novel became badly tarnished. If James himself remained politely admiring toward George Eliot, younger writers were scathingly dismissive. As formalist values consolidated in the first two decades of the twentieth century, *Middlemarch* became an example of How Not To Do It. It came to stand as the representative novel of a Victorian sensibility that seemed the great obstacle to literary renovation. "George Eliot was not ignorant," conceded Arnold Bennett (1909), "but she was too preoccupied by moral questions to be a first-class artist." Ford Madox Ford (1908) concurred, describing her as

great enough to impose herself upon her day; she probably never sought, though she certainly found, the popularity of sensationalism. Taking herself with an enormous seriousness, she dilated upon sin and its results, and so found the easy success of the popular preacher who deals in horrors. She desired that is to say, to be an influence: she cared in her heart very little whether or not she would be considered an artist.

For George Bernard Shaw, the problem of George Eliot was not that she failed to be a formalist, but that she succeeded in being a scientist. He wrote to one correspondent that she "was like the released Bastille prisoners: she was rescued from the chains of Evangelical religion & immediately became lost, numbed & hypnotized by 'Science'." From Shaw's point of view, the problem with George Eliot's cult of science (as opposed to his own) was that it led her to a "useless, dispiriting, discouraging fatalism" (1899). In complaining of Henry James's play *The Saloon*, Shaw wrote and asked the author, "What do you want to break men's spirits for? Surely George Eliot did as much of that as is needed" (1909). T. S. Eliot shared little with Shaw, but on this question they were as one. In *After Strange Gods* the author of *Middlemarch* is said to exhibit "the dreary rationalism of the epoch" (1934).

In *Aspects of the Novel* (1927), E. M. Forster develops a comparison between George Eliot and Dostoevsky, pointing out that both were raised with Christian beliefs, that both broke from their faith, and that both remained imbued with a Christian moral fervor. But having drawn this comparison, Forster then quotes a long passage from each writer in order to show the radical difference between them. "What is the difference in these passages," asks Forster, "a difference that throbs in every phrase? It is that the first writer is a preacher, and the second a prophet." The description of *Middlemarch* as the work of a mere "preacher" became prominent in early twentieth-century criticism, and it meant that the novel became as uninteresting to those who sought moral prophets as it was to those who aspired to be literary formalists.

The modernizing postures of James, Shaw, Ford, Bennett, Forster, and T. S. Eliot varied extravagantly, but they each found reason to identify George Eliot as the bearer of an obsolete sensibility that needed to be swept from their path. The combined force of their critique resulted in a sharp devaluation of George Eliot through the first half of the twentieth century. In the first several decades she was the object of the kind of attacks catalogued here. In the next decades she was more forgotten than vilified. "I must say," remarked George Orwell (1948), "I've never been able to read G.E. herself."

In 1962, at the age of fifty-eight Evelyn Waugh wrote to Nancy Mitford that he was "reading *Middlemarch* for the first time, with enjoyment." But a few weeks later he corrected his impression: "*Middlemarch* wasn't any good really." These offhand comments by Orwell and Waugh suggest just how diminished the once titanic novel had come to seem, no longer something one had to confront, now scarcely something one had to read.

Both the extravagant hostility and the cool distance have complex causes, and among them is a pronounced dislike, not just of a Victorian novelist, but of a Victorian female novelist. A novelistic preacher would be bad enough, but a woman preaching in fiction becomes a kind of monster. The caricature dominating images of George Eliot typically drew her as a social or biological aberration, a female who failed to coincide with her biology, an overly ambitious woman who rashly ventured into the male domain without being able to escape the liabilities of her sex. Henry James's dismissal of Will Ladislaw as a "woman's man" suggests the instinctive recourse to gender as a principle of explanation. Arnold Bennett (1896) commits himself to a more expansive view. Writing of George Eliot's style, he describes it as "too rank to have an enduring vitality. People call it 'masculine'. Quite wrong! It is downright, aggressive, sometimes rude, but genuinely masculine, never. On the contrary it is transparently feminine — feminine in its lack of restraint, its wordiness, and the utter absence of feeling for form which characterizes it."

Virginia Woolf enjoys pride of place in the twentieth-century reception of *Middlemarch*. During a period of often vituperative critique, Woolf was virtually unique among the modernists in acknowledging the splendor of "the mature *Middlemarch*, the magnificent book which with all its imperfections is one of the few English novels written for grown-up people." Woolf's opinion first appeared in an essay of 1919, but it was not until well after the Second World War that her strategy for reading the novel became widely imitated. It was Woolf's particular interest to separate George Eliot from the homogenous Victorian ideology projected by the modernists, to rescue her *difference* from her contemporaries, specifically to rescue her as a woman. Tellingly, she observes that "her critics, who have been, of course, mostly of the opposite sex, have resented, half consciously perhaps, her deficiency in a quality which is held to be supremely desirable in women. George Eliot was not charming; she was not strongly feminine." With this turn toward the question of gender, Woolf prepares not only for a rehabilitation of *Middlemarch*, but also for a new style of reading that would become prominent in our time. To see the novel not as the dull expression of an age of dullness, but as the precipitate of complex forces, especially the forces of gender conflict, is to open it to new and powerful interrogations.

In *The Great Tradition* (1948), F. R. Leavis quotes Woolf's praise of George Eliot and, without adopting her feminism, aligns himself with the strong endorsement of *Middlemarch*. There can be no doubt that within the academic community, Leavis's book prepared for a striking recovery of George Eliot's reputation, and it did so by directly confuting the terms of the modernist attack. Indeed it was part of Leavis's mission to free the achievement of modernism both from its strong technical obsessions and its cosmopolitan indifference to national traditions. Form for Leavis was no independent aesthetic value; it was, when properly appreciated, a component of the essentially moral project that gave prose fiction its dignity. In *The Great Tradition* Leavis staunchly defends George Eliot from James's charge that her fiction achieved no significant formal distinction. "Is there any great novelist," he asks, "whose preoccupation with 'form' is not a matter of his responsibility towards a rich human interest, or complexity of interests, profoundly realized? – a responsibility involving, of its very nature, imaginative sympathy, moral discrimination and judgment of relative human value." The answer, of course, is No, and the very language of the question establishes an affinity between Leavis and George Eliot. Far from seeking a break between Victorian and modern achievements, *The Great Tradition* insists on a continuous legacy stretching from Jane Austen to D. H. Lawrence, and within that tradition, *Middlemarch*, in its deep Englishness and in its deep moral seriousness, occupies a place of grandeur.

Just two years later, in another highly influential piece of criticism, V. S. Pritchett describes the antagonism to George Eliot as a thing of the past: "We dismiss the late-Victorian reaction from her work; our fathers were bored by her because they were importuned by her mind; she was an idol with feet of clay and, what was worse, appeared to write with them. . . And yet when we read a few pages of any of her books now, we notice less the oppression of her lectures and more the spaciousness of her method, the undeterred illumination which her habit of mind brings to human nature." Pritchett goes on to write that "No Victorian novel approaches *Middlemarch* in its width of reference, its intellectual power, or the imperturbable spaciousness of its narrative."

At the end of the decade Iris Murdoch wrote a series of essays that strongly complemented the revaluations of Leavis and Pritchett. Murdoch began with the premise that modern fiction is incontestably inferior to the achievement of the nineteenth century, and in wanting to explain our century's aesthetic failure, she develops a coherent attack on the modern orthodoxy. The fundamental difficulty, she argues, is an attenuated understanding of fictional character, the persistent tendency being to abstract character from a dense social web, to lift the solitary ego out of its background and its context: "The hero is alone, with no company, or with only parts of himself for company." What is more, there is no autonomy granted to the character; there is instead a "ruthless subjection of characters to the will of their author." Put epigrammatically, "What we have lost is persons." And it is in the context of this loss and the general impoverishment of prose fiction that Murdoch argues the case for the nineteenth century and for George Eliot. The placing of the ego within a rich network of social relations, the creation not of solitary selves but of a plurality of persons within a wide expanse, and above all the invention of characters who do not merely reflect the dispositions of the author but obey dispositions of their own – this is seen not only as the grand accomplishment of nineteenth-century fiction but as the distinctive virtue of the novel as a genre. Murdoch takes violent exception to T. S. Eliot's critique, calling it "unpardonable, that he should cast his vote against George Eliot. For she, at a level at times almost equal to that of Tolstoy, displays that godlike capacity for so respecting and loving her characters as to make them exist as free and separate beings.'' Murdoch, along with Leavis and Pritchett, thus established the terms for a surpassing of an aesthetic orthodoxy and the rehabilitation of George Eliot.

In large part, then, the novel's present high reputation is due to the waning of modernist ferocity with its more austere standards of acceptability. Now that the modern aesthetic is so frequently mocked, rebutted, or ignored, there is no shame in tasting the pre-modern pleasures of *Middlemarch*. What is still more striking is the element of congruity between the pre- and post-modern, where the latter is understood not in a polemical or sectarian sense, but simply as a rough historical discrimination. The indifference to the demands of formal unity, the concern with problems of gender, the attention to the relationships between historical context and immediate experience, the interest in the ambiguities of the discontinuous self — these are as central to the workings of George Eliot's novel as they are to the workings of contemporary critical consciousness. No one would mistake *Middlemarch* for a work by Thomas Pynchon. Still, both *Middlemarch* and *Gravity's Rainbow* (1973) are notable for their willingness to sprawl past the borders of aesthetic purity established by the tradition associated with James. Indeed, it is not so much for its particular moral values, or its historical realism, or its scientism, that contemporary readers seem to respond to the novel; but precisely for its sheer sprawling press into many lives and many possibilities.

Within the academic community the present turn toward a ''new historicism'' repeats many of the gestures of George Eliot's older historicism. The refusal to isolate any person, any place, any event, any text; the insistence on situating every part within some larger whole; the resolve to interpret experience in the terms of historical change; all this links *Middlemarch* to the contemporary recovery of history. The current critical desire to uncover the subtle interplay between text and context is anticipated by a novel that is so profoundly *about* the powers of context.

It would be too much to say that the reception history of *Middlemarch* has reached its own happy ending, but living as we must in the everlasting middle, we can at least say that our age is one happy chapter in the posthumous history of the book. After a series of assaults on the reputation of *Middlemarch*, beginning soon after its triumphant publication, the novel has recovered a prestige that seems unlikely to diminish in the sightable future. It has become a landmark in the sense that this series implies, a stable part of the cultural map that may be queried, reconsidered, and reinterpreted without losing its historical preeminence. And now we, academic critics or common readers, are ourselves the context for a novel that teaches how context can strangle or caress, can cut short the reach of genius or let it stretch its long limbs.

Guide to further reading

The standard academic edition of *Middlemarch* has now become the Clarendon Edition (Oxford 1986) edited by David Carroll, but for the purposes of the general reader, the Riverside edition (Boston 1956), the Penguin English Library edition (Harmondsworth 1965), and the Norton Critical Edition (New York 1977) remain serviceable.

The standard biography is *George Eliot: A Biography* (Oxford 1968) by Gordon S. Haight. It has been complemented by two more strongly interpretative works whose emphases are shown in their subtitles, *George Eliot: The Emergent Self* (New York 1975) by Ruby V. Redinger and *George Eliot: A Woman of Contradictions* (London 1989) by Ina Taylor. In his *Golden Codgers: Some Biographical Speculations* (London 1973) Richard Ellmann raised some intriguing and controversial biographical possibilities in a discussion of "Dorothea's Husbands." The recently published *A George Eliot Chronology* (London 1989) by Timothy Hands provides an extremely useful digest of the life.

Gordon S. Haight has edited the nine volumes of *The George Eliot Letters* (New Haven 1954–78) and has also assembled the one-volume *Selections from George Eliot's Letters* (New Haven 1985). Useful additional resources include the *Essays of George Eliot*, ed. Thomas Pinney (London 1963); *George Eliot: A Writer's Notebook 1854–1879 and Uncollected Writings*, ed. Joseph Wisenfarth (Charlottesville 1981); *Quarry for "Middlemarch"*, ed. Anna Kitchel (Berkeley 1950); and *George Eliot's "Middlemarch" Notebooks: A Transcription*, eds. John Clark Pratt and Victor A, Neufeldt (Berkeley 1979).

The modern academic consideration of *Middlemarch* can be dated from two works of the late 1940s: F. R. Leavis's *The Great Tradition* (London 1948) and Mark Schorer's essay, "Fiction and the Matrix of Analogy," first published in the *Kenyon Review* of 1949. Leavis's strong claims for the moral seriousness of *Middlemarch* and for its lofty place in an English tradition gave a strong validating authority to the resurgence of critical interest in the next two decades. Schorer's attempt to apply formalist principles that had been successful in the reading of poetry served to encourage more extensive treatment of technical concerns in the novel. Barbara Hardy's *The Novels of George Eliot: A Study in Form* (London 1959) and W. J. Harvey's *The Art of George Eliot* (London 1961) represented influential examinations of the fictional technique of *Middlemarch* and securely established the formal interest of the work. At the same time both works elaborated and revised Leavis's apprehension of its moral force. Two accomplished later formal studies are Hilda M. Hulme's "The Language of the Novel," in *"Middlemarch"*: *Critical Approaches to the Novel* (London 1967) and Robert Kiely's "The Limits of Dialogue in *Middlemarch*," in *The Worlds of Victorian Fiction*, ed. Jerome H. Buckley (Cambridge, Mass. 1975). Of the numerous books and essays that descend from the early achievements of Leavis, Hardy and Harvey, the chapter on *Middlemarch* in U. C. Knoepflmacher's *Laughter and Despair*: *Readings in Ten Novels of the Victorian Era* (Berkeley 1971) should be singled out as a distinguished refinement of both the moral and formal approaches.

A second strain of reading grew out of the scholarly researches of Gordon S. Haight, whose edition of the letters began appearing in the mid-fifties. The abundance of new materials stimulated a more precise attention to context well represented in Jerome Beaty's 1957 article, "History by Indirection: the Era of Reform in *Middlemarch*", *Victorian Studies*, I (1957) and his book *"Middlemarch" from Notebook to Novel* (Urbana 1960). Bernard Paris's *Experiments in Life*: *George Eliot's Quest for Values* (Detroit 1965) represented an early attempt to offer a comprehensive presentation of the intellectual historical background of the fiction. The publication of the Haight biography in 1968 accelerated the efforts of historically minded critics. The early 1970s saw such helpful work as Michael York Mason's essay *"Middlemarch* and Science: Problems of Life and Mind," *Nineteenth-Century Fiction*, 25 (1971) and James F. Scott's essay "George Eliot, Positivism and the Social Vision of *Middlemarch*," *Victorian Studies*, 16 (1972).

A more recent outgrowth of these contextualizing readings has been a series of book-length studies that place the novel in sustained and detailed relation to aspects of its nineteenth-century milieu. In *George Eliot and Community*: *A Study in Social Theory and Fictional Form* (Berkeley 1984), Suzanne Graver relies usefully on the sociology of Tönnies in showing how closely George Eliot's work is linked to the transitions in nineteenth-century communal life. Sally Shuttleworth, in *George Eliot and Nineteenth-Century Science*: *The Make-Believe of a Beginning* (Cambridge 1984), establishes the range of contemporary scientific notions that are absorbed in the fiction, while in *Darwin's Plots*: *Evolutionary Narrative in Darwin, George Eliot and Nineteenth-Century Fiction* (London 1983), Gillian Beer demonstrates the pervasive importance of Darwin to the metaphoric and intellectual life of *Middlemarch*. In *George Eliot and Blackmail* (Cambridge, Mass. 1985), Alexander Welsh shows with great subtlety how the recurrence of blackmail in her plots reflects changing conditions of knowledge in an age of mass information.

Several casebooks of criticism have conveniently gathered some of the most important essays. A good place to begin study of the novel is with the collections in *"Middlemarch": Critical Approaches to the Novel*, ed. Barbara Hardy (London 1967); *George Eliot: "Middlemarch,"* ed. Patrick Swindon (London 1972); *This Particular Web: Essays on "Middlemarch,"* ed. Ian Adam (Toronto 1975); *George Eliot's "Middlemarch,"* ed. Harold Bloom (New York 1987) and the Norton Critical Edition of the novel edited by Bert G. Hornback.

Although the turn to literary theory has been far less pronounced in readings of *Middlemarch* than in the readings of other major Victorian novelists such as, for instance, Emily Brontë and Charles Dickens, there have been a few quite significant theoretical studies. The best of the small group are J. Hillis Miller's two essays, "Narrative and History," *ELH*, 41 (1974) and "Optic and Semiotic in *Middlemarch*," in *The Worlds of Victorian Fiction*; Neil Hertz's essay "Recognizing Casaubon," *Glyph: Textual Studies*, 6 (1979); and D. A. Miller's chapter on *Middlemarch* in *Narrative and Its Discontents: Problems of Closure in the Traditional Novel* (Princeton 1981).

Virginia Woolf's feminist understanding of the novel at last found its audience in the 1970s when the emergence of feminist styles of reading changed the terms of approach to *Middlemarch*. Writing on the subject of "Women, Energy and *Middlemarch*," *Massachusetts Review*, 13 (1972), Lee R. Edwards made plain that the relationship of the novel to feminism would be an uneasy and provoking one. The difficulties were well summarized in Zelda Austen's article "Why Feminist Critics Are Angry With George Eliot," *College English*, 37 (1976). There has followed a series of attempts to locate *Middlemarch* within the context of Victorian feminism, most notable among them Kathleen Blake's "*Middlemarch* and the Woman Question," *Nineteenth-Century Fiction*, 31 (1976) and Gillian Beer's important book *George Eliot* (Bloomington 1986). Elaine Showalter's *A Literature of Their Own: British Novelists from Brontë to Lessing* (Princeton 1977) established a coherent lineage of women writers within which to place the fiction of George Eliot. In *The Madwoman in the Attic: The Woman Writer and the Nineteenth-Century Literary Imagination* (New Haven 1979), Sandra M. Gilbert and Susan Gubar offered a strong feminist reading of *Middlemarch* that convincingly established the centrality of gender to our understanding of the work.